MUSE

A "Love & Gospel Music" novel

By Timothy Blaine

ISBN-10: 1507770529
ISBN-13: 978-1507770528

DEDICATION

For the singing cowboy at Civic Center Station

(The spark - the muse)

CONTENTS

Timothy Blaine

ACKNOWLEDGMENTS

EDITED BY

GAMAGE CARTER

Chapter One

Concourse

There he was again, sitting on that filthy cold concrete floor which lies beneath the streets of San Francisco. The subway system for this city is, MUNI, and on a lower level, BART, which connects cities and counties and airports and... well you get the picture, MUNI, for the city, BART, for the whole Bay area. This guy I'm talking about now is always; so far as I could tell on the concourse level just beneath the street above both train levels and usually pretty much in the very same spot at, Powell Street station. He'd probably be considered a street musician by most, although technically he's not since he does his work underground which of course is not a street. He's far from alone in his daily endeavor. San Francisco has got musicians, singers, tap dancers, ventriloquists and, well... Trouble is the good; the bad, and the horrendous are all clanging and banging side by side. A few of them very polished playing on good even classical instruments, probably music students offsetting the cost of books and living in a city such as this. A few more; legitimate street entertainers scratching by with what they do best. Then there's the lion's share; homeless people, just making noise for a buck.

I knew the street life, knew it far better than I cared to, far better than any sane person would... Anyway I want to talk about this dude I kept running into beneath the streets of the city, I'm guessing twenty two, but definitely no more than twenty four years old, probably Black and Latino, or maybe some other combination. His race was not easily determined on sight but he sure did rest easy on the eyes. Not too hard to find good looking people among the young of course, what caught and then held my attention about this particular good-looking young man was when he opened his mouth, or better to say when he played the

instrument. A gifted man with a biological harp lodged in his

throat. No matter his race or nationality this bird could chirp like

no other bird I'd ever encountered on or beneath the streets of

the city. Was it soprano? No soprano is a woman's range, I did

know that much. Maybe it was some kind of rare tenor or

falsetto, I couldn't quite put my finger on it and I couldn't for the

life of me figure why a dude with a voice like that seemed

obsessed with performing church music. Perhaps, the gospel

angle was simply a calculated ploy to loosen the purse of burned

out, 'alms for the poor,' weary pedestrians as they rushed by

making a conscious effort to not make eye contact with the cities

'beggars.'

A beggar, my God, what must it be like for a guy like him;

how good would one have to be to break through and actually be

heard against such a backdrop.

On the next morning as I hurried on my way to my favorite, Starbuck's, which happened to be my favorite spot for people watching and fleshing out new characters for a novel I found the sight of this talented young guy sitting on that filthy floor particularly disturbing. His hands and clothes where a little dirty, not dope fiend dirty, or 'I don't give a shit dirty,' obviously there was some effort at keeping himself together but...

"Hey, was 'up, my man," I said. "Looks like you're getting a slow start today."

"So you finally said something," said the musician setting up his gear. "I see you around here a lot."

"You're good, I mean your sound, you have a hell of a voice, brother, very unique."

"If I'm so good," asked the young man, "why you never put anything in the hat? I see you walking by pretty much every morning, always stopping for just a bit, sometimes even looking back over your shoulder."

"You're right, I've been robbing you blind," I said, pulling a twenty from my front pocket, "feasting on the talent for free." I had to hand him the money since he had yet to place the gold mining hat on the ground.

"Thanks man," he said accepting the bill and shoving it deep into his right sock; which was also very dirty. That settled it; this dude was living on the streets.

"Sure don't see a lot of those around here," he said while switching out old batteries in his battered microphone. "Hopefully this is a sign, that's usually about what I get for the whole morning?"

"You should be getting a lot more for what you do," I said. "You think the setting here might have something to do..."

"Welcome to the world of the one dollar bill. Some of the guys do quite a bit better, especially the ones that look like they don't need the money. Ain't that some shit! Maybe I should take up the fuckin' cello or... Oh shit, here comes, Lucy and Ethel!"

I looked behind me to see two police officers, one male and one female working their way towards us as they used their nightsticks to tap on the shoe soles of several sleeping or passed out men lined up around the subway terminals walls.

"Which ones, Ethel" I asked.

"Woman, she's the sidekick," said the musician, "Lucy's the red-head."

"What's your name, brother?"

"They call me, Spider, and yours?"

"Carson," I said extending my hand, "looks like this might be a great time to go for a cup of coffee, actually I was hoping I'd run into you today."

"Huh," said Spider?

"I want to kick something around with you, brother, could be an opportunity."

"Well, the cops are going to make me keep it moving anyway. What you want to talk about, man?"

"I know a spot," I said, "it's right at the top of the escalator. Here let me help you with your stuff."

Okay so here's the rundown. Spider Man, was a twenty five year old newbie from Fresno, California. He'd been here just over six months but the money he brought with him only lasted about four and a half. The weekly hotel where he'd been staying would only carry him a couple weeks on promises, now they were giving him one more week to pick up his things. After that he like a couple thousand other young people around the city would be carrying everything he owned either on his back or in a cart. This was not a new story. Sooner or later the hard living would bring on the hard drugs. After one or more of the most addictive: heroin, crack or meth sunk their talons into his flesh his chances of realizing any part of his promise would drop to near nothing.

My mission, do something. Maybe, just maybe, it wasn't too late.

Me; my name is, Carson Elliot. I'm thirty four, been living in
the city about thirty three years. There were a couple failed
attempts at NYC. Black, gay, single, unemployed and lovin' it. At
least I'll be, lovin' it, for the next two weeks anyway. That's when I
get the very last unemployment check; no doubt I'll hate it after
that. Oh, I'll still love being Black and gay, maybe even single. It's
just this work thing. No I'm not totally desperate; I won't have to
wait until the fridge and kitchen cabinets are on empty, or hear
the lovely, tap-tap, of an eviction notice being secured at eye
level. My parents own the apartment building where I live and
three others around the city, two bigger ones in Oakland. They've
got more than enough work to keep me busy for the next ten or
twenty or thirty years. Trouble is I'm just not that interested. I've
got my own dreams, none of which include changing out old toilet
seats, setting out garbage bins or getting cussed the fuck out

every time I politely mention that someone's rent was a little overdue."

"Thanks for the coffee," said Spider as we took seats at an outside table, "so you've been waiting for me?"

"Yeah, I've wanted to talk to you for a while now," I said, "the timing just never seemed right. I'm a little shy and there's not much of a break between your songs."

"I'm not gay, Carson."

"What! Don't flatter yourself, dude," I said. "Anyway, me wanting you is not something either of us needs to be worrying about, trust me on that one."

"Believe it or not, I get quite a few offers," said Spider, "even down there."

"It's the face and youth, brother, which I'm sorry to say are fleeting even under the best of conditions. I wanted to talk about something at least a little more under our control."

"So you brought me up here to cheer me up about the inevitability of my vanishing youth, that it?'

"Actually, I initially wanted to talk about your music," I said, "I know some people. But now, I don't know, looks like you might have a few more pressing issues."

"Really, like what?"

"The duffle bag, you're clothes are, well... I mean no disrespect man, but..."

"So you think I'm dirty," said Spider pushing his chair back a little, "have you gotten a good whiff yet? I'm sure I probably stink a little too. Forgot the bubble bath this morning, sorry!"

"I didn't ask you up here to insult you, man."

"Just say what's on your mind, dude! You don't want to see me pissed off!"

"Relax, man, I lived in Golden Gate Park for two years when I was your age, which wasn't all that long ago. I'm not judging you Spider; I just really like your voice, man. I'd like to try to help you."

"You're in the music industry?"

"Nope."

"Own or manage a club," he asked, "oh, I got it, you're a choir director. Is that it Carson? Am I right about it?"

"No, look, man," I said, "my parents have a few properties around the city. I'm guessing you need a place. Maybe we could help each other out."

"I don't understand," said Spider, "I thought this was about music."

"Trust me, brother, you're never going to be taken seriously playing for loose change on that concourse. We need to get you into a venue where that sound you make can be appreciated."

"We?"

"Yeah, you and me," I said, "I've been thinking about this for a couple weeks now, so yeah, I guess you could say I've been checking you out."

"So what's in it for you, Carson, and be honest, man."

"Let's just say you inspire me."

"I think we need to say a little more than that," he said, "why bother?"

"Okay, okay, so I'm a writer."

"You want to interview me," he asked, "you're a professional journalist?"

"Well technically I think you need to be making a living to call yourself a professional anything. No, actually I'm a novelist, I write about criminals and mysterious circumstances."

"How many?"

"Five, I was working on a sixth until...," I said. "Well, I just started working on something new. I know, you're probably wondering what the hell that has to do with your music, right?"

"Naw, I understand, it's the muse thing. Next you're going to tell me that my voice inspires your writing, that it?"

"You know, I mean...," I said my eyes bulging slightly; "I mean it's just the strangest damn thing I've ever heard of. The second time I heard you singing "I know it was the blood," down in that concourse... dude, I must have heard that song sung a hundred times by nearly as many people, but I never... It was like I could almost see the blood of Christ running down over the subway tile down there. That was what I had been missing, my readers needed to see, to feel... I went home and deleted most of what I had been working on over the last few months. I immediately started a new approach and it's so much better, man. I feel like I owe you, brother."

"Well, here we go again," said Spider, "believe it or not this is not the first time I've heard that. I've even worked with a couple dudes. Of course pretty much anybody or anything for that matter can be somebody's muse for creating something, there's just this thing about my family and writers. My patriarchal grandmother, who was a black woman, married three times. All three of her husbands were writers, two of them novelists."

"So what do you consider yourself, Spider," I asked, "I mean as far as...?"

"I'm Black," he said, "well technically, I'm Black and Jewish. My mom is Jewish, not very maternal though, I hardly know her. I was raised by my dad's people."

"Not by him," I asked.

"Dude, if you must know it all. I'm twenty five years old. My dad has been locked up for nineteen of those years. Actually he lives here in the Bay Area too. He's a lifer at San Quentin."

"I'm sorry, man. You get along with your family?"

"I guess so," he said, "except pretty much everybody in my family thinks I'm ether stupid or crazy as hell for coming up here. They're pretty much all die hard suburbanites. San Francisco might as well be on a different planet."

"It's a pretty bold move, man. This city can be kinda hard on newcomers. So what's your plan Spider, why San Francisco?"

"Why not, I mean I stayed home until I was twenty four years old, it was way pass time to get off the toilet. I like it here man, I'm not going back."

"Kind of a rough start?"

"Let's talk about you, Carson," said Spider, "you said you were waiting for me?"

"Okay, so here's what I'm thinking, Spider Man. My parents have been holding the job of manager of all the SF properties for over a month. The work is backed up and even if by some miracle I do get caught up, it never stops. I can't write twenty words before the damn phone is ringing!"

"You've done the job before?"

"Yeah, off and on since I was a teenager," I said. "Look, it's not really such a bad deal. They always pay me well; plus the apartment."

"You get free rent?" said Spider! "Damn, I wish I had your problems."

"That's the thing, man. There's a pretty decent space in the basement. Maintenance man used to live there years ago so I'm pretty sure it's legal, but lately they've just been storing sinks and shit down there."

"You want me to come and work for you, Carson; you're offering me a job?"

"It's a chance to get stable, man," I said, "It's not hard work, Spider, mostly painting, keeping the common area's clean, changing light bulbs, shit like that."

"How much does it pay?"

"Will it pay; I'll have to sell my parents on the idea. And of course you'd get the studio."

"So this is not a real offer then?"

"Oh, it's real alright; I wouldn't play those kinds of games with you, brother. You say the word, and we'll get your stuff over there right now. I'll deal with my parents."

"Okay, so that would be a 'hell yeah, I'll take the job, are you kidding me!"

"It's a sweet setup for a musician, man. Very quiet, tenants can't hear anything down there."

"So what's this about you knowing 'some people' in the music industry, Carson?"

"We'll get to that," I said. "Let's get you over to the

building. We've got some work to do to get it ready.

Chapter Two

Duboce Triangle

"Nice," said Spider as we entered the well maintained twenty unit red brick structure in the city's, Duboce Triangle, neighborhood. "So your folks are rich?"

"They do okay," I said. "My dad's a corporate attorney; he's kept long hours for as far back as I retain memory. My mom works all the real estate. She'll be our boss, but doesn't come around much. Strangely enough she actually prefers Oakland. Anyway they moved across the bay a few years back."

"Retain memory, wow," he said, "that a little of the rich college kid coming out?"

"Ha ha ha," I laughed, "you're a sharp dude. I wrote a little novella called 'Retained Memory,' for a creative writing class I took once, that's all that's coming out."

"So you live up stairs?"

"Yeah, building has four floors; I'm on the top floor all the way in the back. Let's go get cleaned up, we'll eat, and then I'll show you the studio."

He spent the first week sleeping on my couch as we worked diligently on the space in the basement.

"Dude, I read your first novel last night," said Spider! "All of it; didn't finish until one in the morning. Man, I haven't done that since fuckin' high school. You're good. I mean like, damn, you're a great writer, Carson! And I'm not just talking about your story telling, it's your prose dude. I absolutely could not put it down!"

"What; how did you...?"

"Kindle download," he said, "$2.99, best three bucks I ever spent."

"Brother you didn't have to..."

"Yes I did, you've done so much for me, dude, of course I was curious."

"Are you just being nice, Spider Man," I said? "Did you really like the book that much? We're talking about "A Perfect Place to Hide," right?"

"Yep, that's the first one, teenage killers hiding out in Golden Gate Park. You wrote it when you were about my age, damn. I know you're saying it's all a work of fiction, but I don't know... seems like there's a lot of..."

"Most of the story is fictional."

"But you really did move into the park for two years?"

"Those first novels," I said, "okay, so like with a lot of authors, first books tend to blur the line. I put everything I knew, thought, or imagined in that first one, and yes I tried to walk a mile in most of the character's shoes. But as far as I know I didn't run into any pack of teenage murderers on the run."

"You got a paper back copy around," he asked, "one we can mess up a little? I want to show you something."

"Sure hope it's not some typo or print errors," I said, "that was a long time ago, man."

"No, the book is fantastic, brother. Even if there is a wrinkle or two, which I didn't see any, I wouldn't change even as much as a comma. It's just a little hobby I have."

"Okay, so sure," I said, "I just happen to have a few dozen unsold copies under my..."

"How about a yellow highlighter," he yelled as I left the room, "and black coffee if you have it! This is going to blow your mind Carson, I promise."

'*What was this dude up to,*' I wondered, '*surely he wasn't planning on defacing my first born child right in front of me.*'

"Okay, my friend," he said; as I stepped back into the room, carrying the most used copy of the novel I could find in one hand, a cup of coffee in the other, highlighter in my shirt pocket, just as instructed. "I think we can probably agree that you're an extremely talented writer," he continued, "and if there is one thing I know; its music, I can't write it, but I sure as hell know when I'm hearing beautiful lyrics."

He then began making lines in my book, lots and lots of yellow lines. I should have been asking him what the hell he thought he was doing, instead I sat quietly in a chair across from him thinking, *my God he's beautiful.*

"Alright, I've got a question," he said, "It's something I've wanted to ask of a lot of book writers, all kinds of writers actually. Don't you guys like money?"

"Look, Spider Man, I've got a lot of work to..."

"I'm serious, dude! You can sit down and write four or five hundred pages of beautiful prose and dialogue, what is that, eighty, ninety thousand fuckin' words?"

"I thought you said you liked the book," I said. "Okay, so yeah, it's a lot of words and a whole lot of damn work."

"And your compensation?"

"What, look kid..."

"Come on, man," he said, "how many books you sell this year? Fuck it, let's take the whole ten years you've been writing novels? Throw out a number, Carson, don't be embarrassed."

"You're pissing me off now. Game over!"

"One, one and a half pages, that's all I'm trying to say, man," he said suddenly taking me by both of my shoulders. "Carson Elliot, you write beautifully, it's a gift from God. Please, just let me show you what I hear in your writing, let me show you the music, brother."

Okay, so let's get something straight, I did not bring that man here for any reason other than what was plainly stated on the day of that initial proposal. I was not just blowing smoke up his ass when I told him I thought he possessed a rare talent. All I wanted to do was help him. There was good reason to believe I could do just that, not just with a little legit work and a place to hang his hat. I really did know some people, actually some fairly big people in the gospel music industry. Let me give you a little back story here. About ten years back my parents and I had fallen out big time. I had just graduated from, State, and informed them that four years had been enough college for me. Well, you could probably have fried hamburger on the top of my dad's head. I thought he was going to hit me! We're not talking about a father disciplining an unruly child; I was twenty four years old. I thought my dad was going to knock my fuckin' lights out. He said I had ripped him off for over a hundred thousand dollars. When I told him of my plans to pursue a career as a mystery writer he did take a swing, then another, and then... Fortunately I was young and in a whole hell of a lot better shape than him. Before he could beat me down he'd have to catch me first.

A few days later my then boyfriend, Charley Franklin, called the house looking for me. He was no doubt a little hysterical since he hadn't seen or heard from me in three days. According to, Charley; after a few heated words he'd informed my dad that he was my lover and unless he got some very good answers as to my whereabouts he was going to contact the police.

Thanks a lot, Charley Franklin! That's all I needed was to be outed to my parents by your nasty pink... Anyway I just wasn't that into, Charley, which would explain why I didn't bother to call him. After a few days of couch surfing and borrowing socks and t-shirts I did however call my mother. She said she'd meet me at the, McDonalds, at the corner of Haight and Stanyan. We had a nice long talk at the end of which she walked me out into the parking lot, clicked open the trunk of her Mercedes; then got in the driver's seat and started the car. In the trunk were several

large black trash bags containing my clothes.

I just sat there in a daze on a curb in that, McDonalds,

parking lot for what seemed like hours. Sure, I knew they'd be

pissed about my announcement, especially my super ambitious,

egomaniacal, bald headed, republican father. He was already

trying to dot my eyes about school and my lack of interest in his

chosen profession. Then comes that stupid ass call from, Charley

Franklin. Fuck, what the hell was that? The asshole thought my

parents had killed me; then got rid of the body because I didn't

want to become a lawyer? I gotta tell you the thought that I'd

ever dropped my drawers with that stupid ass... Anyway, after a

while a pack of grunge kids wandered into the lot. "Hey, you guys

want some clothes?" I yelled across the lot.

"What's the style, man," yelled an overweight, pimply

faced, redheaded kid of no more than sixteen? He looked like he

hadn't had a bath, showered or been hosed down in months.

"We're kinda' particular about what we put on our bodies, man!"

It looked like most of what they were wearing had been pulled from a garbage disposal then drug across miles and miles of oil, hot tar and bad road before they patched it back to something that could be called clothing. "There are a couple biker jackets and boots in here." I said as I rummaged through a couple of the bags taking only the few essentials that would fit into my backpack. When my parents calmed the fuck down and let me back in the house I'd tell them I'd been robbed and beaten, maybe even butt raped too! Serve them right for treating me that way. Besides school was over, I deserved all new shit anyway.

Kinda lost in that moment, I wandered across the street to, Golden Gate Park, where I scored a few joints, dug my iPod out of the backpack, laid my head against a big rock, closed my eyes and at least for the moment, forgot about my troubles.

"Dude, dude, wake up," said a tall black dreadlocked, stranger! "Come on, brother, rise and shine!"

"What...who...what...," I stammered coming awake. "What the fuck, man!"

"This is a public service announcement," said a second stranger, this one white, just as tall, with powder blue eyes, and an ash blond ponytail that reached the low part of his back. He was cupping his hands as if speaking through a foghorn. "You have just been ripped off, citizen!"

By instinct I looked around for my leather backpack, it was gone. In that same instant I realized my headphones were still in my ears yet attached to nothing. "Dammit," I yelled! "My phone and my fuckin' iPad were in there!"

"Thought we'd wake you before somebody got a good look at the watch," said the white one. "You do realize where you are?"

"Dude, you're layin' out here wearin' a fuckin' Rolex," said the black one! "You're lucky you didn't lose a damn arm!"

"Did you see them," I asked?

"Naw, well kinda, look it could've been anybody, man. Ryan Prescott," said the white one offering me a hand up. "And this is my buddy Dallas."

"Thanks," I said accepting his hand. "Guess this makes me the victim of a crime; think I should bother with the cops?"

"They're just a bunch of desperate hungry kids, man." said Dallas, "Why make things worse. It'd just bring extra heat on the place."

"Your shit is long gone, dude." said Ryan, "Probably already traded for a few dime bags."

"Besides," said Dallas, "you look like you can afford to buy plenty more crap anyway."

"I guess I could sell the watch," I said, my current circumstances coming back into focus, "Damn, they even got my fucking weed!"

"Well, it just so happens…" said Ryan pulling a few joints from his right front pocket. "I got, Wowie, Ganja or Skunk. Name your poison, dude."

"Damn," I said. "You carry all that around in your front pocket! You guys in the business?"

"Now wouldn't that be about the craziest damn thing you ever heard of," said Dallas shooting Ryan a look. "Why in the hell would anybody in that line of work be carrying the shit around in their front fuckin' pocket?"

"Don't start, Dallas," said Ryan. "Let's take a walk, citizen."

The three of us walked down narrow paths, through clusters of trees and tall weeds, eventually coming into a small trampled grass clearing. There were a few, degraded McDonalds' bags, beer cans, dirty clothes and empty condom wrappers so guess we were secluded enough to not have to worry about parks and recreation or the cops walking up on us.

So this is how I met my friends, Ryan and Dallas. They weren't in the music or any other industry back then. Ryan Prescott was extremely good-looking; actually Dallas was fine as hell too, just a little less my type. To be honest Dallas looked a lot like me, which was definitely not my type. I'm one of those that need a little contrast. Anyway we got high. Actually we got very high and stayed that way until the park got dark. They had all but offered me a spot on their floor for the night until I made some kind of off handed remark about the roundness of Ryan's butt cheeks. I know, rude, crude, and disrespectful, but as I said we were all three as high as a kite, at least I didn't get punched in the face. After I saw Dallas's reaction to the comment and my wandering eyes, I was not surprised when the forthcoming invitation never arrived. So, they were lovers. I guess I was somehow supposed to know that.

Anyway, I had several options for temporary lodgings. After all I'd been born and raised in the city, had plenty of friends and relatives. Hell, the, San Francisco State, campus was just a few stops up on, MUNI; where I could easily crash at half a dozen different places. I could even call up, Charley Frank... Anyway, I didn't call anybody, just talked a little and did a whole lot of listening to pretty much everybody I came across. When Ryan and Dallas showed up the next afternoon I had pretty much circled back around to the same spot where they had left me. I was quick to apologize for the night before, and Ryan was quick to whip out a few more joints.

"So you guys are together," I said after the first drag. "Again, I'm real sorry for... you never said anything."

"What's your story Carson?" said Dallas, "You haven't changed clothes. It's abnormal to wear Abercrombie more than one day."

"Yeah, I hung out here last night."

"You got a place to go, man?" asked Ryan.

"If I choose to," I said. "Look man, my parents packed up all my shit and dropped it off here yesterday."

"Damn," said Dallas, "they put you out?"

"Again," I said. "I think this is either the fifth or sixth time. Whenever they run out of words, which is saying a lot in the case of, the Republican, they get out the trash bags."

"The Republican," asked Ryan.

"That's my dad," I said. "He wants to be white."

"Joining, the Republican Party," said Dallas, "yeah, I guess that would make since."

"Claims it's all about the smaller role of government, but... anyway these expulsions usually only last a day or so. At least, that's the way it always worked before. Technically I haven't lived there in about four years though."

"You said your clothes were there," said Dallas, "you moved back in?"

"Yeah, school's out," I said, "both the roommates moved back to their home states, our apartment was a sublet. What about, you two, what do you do?"

"Music," they said in unison.

"You're in a band," I asked, "have I heard of, you guys."

"I doubt it," said Ryan, "actually around here we're a lot better known for the product you're presently sampling."

"So I was right," I said, "you guys are selling."

"Not so loud," said Dallas. "As soon as these dudes catch on we're out of here. There are more rats in just this part of the park than there are slimy things in the Pacific."

So at the time the three of us met at, Golden Gate Park, ten long years back they were selling weed. I later found out it was Dallas who was doing most of the selling; Ryan was just a big ol' pot head like me. The three of us became fast friends and started hanging out all over, the Haight. Several offers were made for me to squeeze into their tiny apartment on, Haight Street, until my parents came around or I found a place to live. I declined and decided to let them in on a little secret.

"I've got my story," I said, "I'm sure of it, guys."

"The book?" asked Ryan. "You've got an idea for the book?"

"Don't mean to be a downer, dude," said Dallas, "but do you really think this is the right time to start writing fiction?"

"Oh, give it a break, Dallas," said Ryan. "Anytime is the right time if the inspiration is there. So what are you thinking, man?"

"Well, it's a novel," I said, "that's all I'm saying."

"Come on, dude," said Ryan!

"Okay, a mystery inspired by the characters in and around the park," I said, "and that really is all I'm saying, Ryan. Listen thanks for the food and shower guys. I really need to get back over there now."

"Hold on a minute," said Dallas, "I need to say something to you, man."

"What's up?" I asked.

"It's about the product, Carson," he said, "dude you're getting high way too much."

"Hey," said Skye, "like we're not! What's this about, Dallas? The man's a writer, he just announced that he's found something to write about, and this is your reaction?"

"The dude can be making six figures in a couple more years," yelled Dallas, "and he wants to write books, does anybody even read fuckin' novels anymore! Now, we've been let in on a big earth shattering secret, it's a novel based on the lives of a bunch of fucked up hungry kids living in the damn park! Talk about a fuckin' best seller!"

"Oh, shut up, Dallas," said Ryan. "You're sounding like a real asshole right now! As if we know what the hell we're doing either. We don't even know what kind of music we want to do, man."

"All I'm saying is that he needs to get out of that fuckin' park, Ryan, it can be hella dangerous out there. Believe me, if those kids had any other options they wouldn't be freezing their little asses off sleeping in the fuckin' bushes."

"That's your opinion," I said. "You forget the sixties, all the history of this place? Look, this is my life, dude! You don't like my choices, fuck you! I'll get the shit someplace else!"

"Hold on, Carson," said Skye grabbing his jacket, "I'll walk over with you. That's real fucking nice, Dallas." He said slamming the door behind us.

"He's a good dude, Carson," said Skye, "I hope you understand, it's not you. He's crazy about you, calls you his little brother."

"Yeah, I can see that!"

"It's the guilt, man," said Skye. "That man is in the wrong line of work."

Well, Ryan and Dallas did finally figure out what kind of music they wanted to do, and when they came out with it, well, damn! I just never saw it coming, gospel music. I mean it's not like I have anything against gospel music, in fact I was raised on it, even managed to butcher a few notes and chords myself while in our church's youth choir. That was before the church hired a new music director. Miss Bennett figured out what the problem was pretty quick after her first rehearsal. Me and three others were out. I'll be honest. The youth choir did get a whole lot better after that. Anyway who would have thought that Ryan Prescott and Dallas Jordan, excuse me, they now go by Skye Davenport and Dallas Withers (don't ask) would record the biggest selling Gospel Music CD in the history of the genre. I mean we're talking about my weed connection here.

Dallas is the voice, and that Ryan, I mean Skye, well I'm just gonna say straight out, he is, at least in my head the best songwriter, in any genre, living.

Chapter Three

Dallas Withers

"Hey, guess who?"

"Carson," said Dallas smiling through the phone line after being put through by his secretary. "Dude, you think I'd ever forget that queeny ass voice? Please tell me you're calling to tell me you're coming to LA."

"Actually, I'm here in the building," I lied, "getting off the elevator right now."

"Bullshit, I fell for that one last year. Whas'up, my man?"

"You sound good, Dallas," I said. "It's been a while, man."

"No shit, way too long brother. Well, you know how it is with us, work, work, eat, sleep, then more damn work. We keep sayin' we're going to get up north at least for a few days, but then, well you know... back to work. When's the new book due for release?"

"Actually, I had to do a huge edit/dump, slid all the way back to chapter two."

"What, you told us a month ago it was going great. That doesn't sound like you, Carson."

"It happens, actually, it's a good thing, Dallas," I said, "you'll see why soon enough."

"Well, I hope you're not giving up on the series, I love those characters, man, they're us."

"I've been getting, "The New York Times." So how's Skye holding up?"

"Well, you know...," he said. "They're in jury selection."

Ryan Prescott a.k.a. Skylar Davenport's, father, Mr. Raymond Prescott was about to go on trial in Manhattan for four counts of first degree murder, in the deaths of his wife, their butler, maid and a private detective under her hire.

"Damn, it's just so hard to believe all that shit really happened."

"A whole lot stranger than fiction, right," he said? "Well, you can't write any books about it, Carson, there's been way too much written about it all ready and the damn trial hasn't even started yet. Like there's even a snow balls' chance... Bloodsuckin' lawyers are just going to burn through whatever's left. Then they'll throw away the key anyway. Man, this is all so fuckin' hard on Skye, Heather and the kids."

"And what about you, how are you doing, Dallas? I mean really, man, talk to me."

"I'm okay," he said, "I just keep working, that's how I cope. So, tell me what's been going on in San Francisco, man. I could really use some distraction right about now."

"I went back to work for my parents," I said. "Can you believe it, damn, I'm thirty four years old, dude; I was supposed to be a fuckin' best seller five times over by now. My publishing deal sucks ass, my dad's trying to get me out of it."

"Offer's still open," said Dallas, "just say the word."

"Naw, I'm not giving up on the writing or the city, Dallas. Besides, I'm an only child. It'll all be mine someday, that is unless I piss them off so bad that they leave it all to charity. There's something I want to kick around with you though, brother."

"Okay."

"I want to put together a demo for you guys to check out."

"You're singing now? I thought you told me you were the wor...."

"The worse, yeah, yeah, I still can't hold a note. I met somebody really special though, Dallas."

"You're in love?"

"Huh? Dude, you know that's not my thing." I said. "Besides, the guy's straight. Anyway, dude, has got the sweetest vocals I've ever heard, man."

"Sweeter than mine?"

"He'll give you diabetes in the eardrums."

"Damn, so who is he?"

"Just a young dude I met on the street, or I should say; under the street," I said. "Actually he's been jamming down at Powell Street Station for a few weeks."

"Wait a minute, Carson, you found this dude hanging out under, Market Street?"

"Yeah, so? Oh come on, Dallas; let's not forget where Joey stumbled across you."

"Don't be a smart ass," he said. "All I'm saying is that it's damn near impossible to turn somebody into a gospel singer if that's not their... Ninety percent of our line-up came out of church settings."

"That's why I called you, man! All this dude does is gospel, brother."

"Really, and he's that good. Sounds like the man really got your attention."

"You know I wouldn't waste your time, man."

"Guess I just figured out how to get your little ass back down here. Look Carson, Skye's up in New York for at least three more weeks, the house is empty and I'm lonely as hell. Why don't you just bring the man down here? Let's see and hear what you're talkin' about."

"You don't want to hear him first?"

"No, give it to me all at once. How's this weekend?"

"Well I..."

"Great, so I'll have Gloria e-mail your confirmations."

"Thanks, Dallas."

"Oh, well... How does he look Dallas? Not that it really matters, but... well it's the young ones that buy."

"Trust me, that's not going to be a problem."

"Spider, hey, Spider Man," I yelled down into the basement! "Hey!"

"Yeah," he yelled back, "somebody's been messing with the cable. We need to build some kind of box around it, man! You need me up there, Carson?"

"I'll come down."

"So, whas'up?"

"We're going to take a little trip, brother," I said beaming. "He wants to meet you, man!"

"L.A.?"

"Tickets already in my in-box, how fast can you finish up? We need to do a little shopping."

"No rehearsal," he asked, "no tape, nothing?"

"Dwayne owns the studio, man. He's the fuckin' CEO! Come on, dude, we've got to do a quick make-over, we're on a plane in two days, not that you need a lot of fixing up, of course. This could be big for you, Spider Man!"

"Guess a haircut wouldn't hurt. Carson, you sure I'm ready for something like this?"

"Yes, I sure as hell am," I said, "brother you stopped me dead in my tracks with that sound you make. I mean I've never heard... Look dude, you're getting a shot at derailing all this starving artist bullshit and you're taking it."

The story of how drug dealing, Dallas Withers, came to be not only a Grammy winning gospel recording artist, but also CEO of Stratton Records could easily have been taken from the pages of an urban fairy tale.

It seems like only yesterday. Of course I'll have to take you back once again to that magical summer in the year, 2004, which is also the summer I came into the picture. Dallas and Skye had been sharing the little studio apartment on Haight Street for about four years, and in fact had actually met each other there inside that apartment. To shorten the story a little, they had been both friends of this other dude, Seth Perkins. Dallas had known the guy since grade school, and in fact had been his best friend for most of their lives growing up in the suburbs of Las Vegas. Seth moved to San Francisco just out of high school, which is where he met Ryan/Skye. They became quick friends then roommates and soon after that Dallas moved to town. Almost immediately they were all three selling weed together. After a few days Seth got busted for direct sales to an undercover police officer working,

Golden Gate Park. From what I understand this is where Ryan and

Dallas's love story really began although it took them quite a

while to admit even to themselves their true feelings. Never mind

that their twin beds had almost immediately been joined and

bolted together.

On one fine afternoon just after they'd made whoopee on

the kitchen floor Dallas headed out to, Polk Street, to make a

couple deliveries and maybe drum up a little street business.

When he returned to the apartment he was very late and very

excited, he had met someone.

Well, basically the guys' lives changed with that chance

meeting between Dallas and Joey White on, Polk Street, that

night. Dallas had always been on the fence about pursuing a

career in gospel music. Joey brought him down off that fence.

Understand we're talking about the coming together of three

extremely talented men here. Joey White had been a

phenomenally successful gospel singer for just over a decade.

Before the tragic death of his partner, Dwayne Brown, the two of them had managed to reinvent him as both an award winning producer and record company executive. Together they'd formed Stratton Records; which quickly became a force to be reckoned with in the gospel music industry. Dallas sang for the man in a taxi twenty minutes after they'd met, the rest is history. At first it was just Joey and Dallas on a plane to, Los Angeles, but Ryan couldn't stay away very long. Separation had confirmed what he had long suspected, he was in love.

Ryan was from a wealthy real-estate family in, Manhattan. Though there was no doubt plenty of money, there was very little else to the family. His father, Raymond Prescott, worked obsessively. He was an only child, and well... Ryan hated his mother. He had good call to hate her.

Now, why in the hell did that dude have to come out of the shower in nothing but a fuckin' towel? Fuck! Everything had been going so well! We were running a little behind schedule, my things were packed into the little Zip Car rental. Spider needed to get a move on, so I went down to help him.

"Hey, sorry, dude," he said, dropping the towel just long enough to slide into his briefs, "just give me a minute. This is hella exciting, man! Damn, I can't believe this is really happening!"

I couldn't take my eyes off him. I was stuck, trying to act normal, trying to talk. What is it about bare flesh? Of course I knew the man was beautiful... those emerald eyes, that smile, the dimples... his body brought tears to my eyes.

"We need to get going," I stammered, picking up one of his canvas bags, "Plane's boarding in an hour." I needed to get out of there and quick. Amazing how denial works in matters of the heart. Though I had only known the Spider Man a few weeks, I had been on the verge of tears since I hung up the phone with Dallas two days prior. What the fuck had I done! Was I really going to escort this man to LA, knowing that more than likely Dallas,

Skye and their whole company were all going to love him? They'd

want to sign him, and also knowing I might very well be falling in...

But wasn't that the plan from the very beginning? I mean this, him

being signed and then moving to LA, this was the plan, right? In

truth I should have realized I was only kidding myself about my

lack of romantic or physical interest in him especially after a trip

to the local Safeway a couple weeks back. The Safeway at the

intersection of Church and Market Streets, often lovingly referred

to as the city's Gayway has never in my recollection been in any

shortage of attractive young people strolling it's aisles, so why had

it seemed they were all staring at us. It certainly wasn't because

of me. At thirty-four my head turning days had already come and

gone. Oh, I'm sure I still catch an eye from time to time, and

getting laid is still not something I have to put a lot of effort into,

but as far as dudes stopping in the aisles at the grocery store to

turn around and gawk at me, well, that was a glory that had

eluded me. Listen, I knew it had to be me, and let me tell you,

feeling jealous and possessive of a dude that had absolutely no physical attraction to me was not a good feeling. I wasn't some naïve teenager having his first crush on Mr. Impossible after all; I knew and played the game well enough. Rule number one, or at least one of the top ten rules, when someone tells you right off the top that they're straight, move-the hell-on. Of course some people actually like the challenge, not me; I'm way too sensitive to be fuckin' around in that emotional waste land.

"I'll wait in the car," I said, "need to feed the meter anyway."

"Be right out Carson." he yelled. "Love you, man!"

'What, what did that mother fucker just say to me?' I thought, *'don't play with me, boy.'* Oh, I know it was just straight dude 'I love you, man' bullshit. Still, I'll admit, I smiled, just a little.

He met us at LAX personally.

"Carson, my man," said Dallas with a big handshake/hug. "Damn, you're aging backwards."

"Right," I said, "well haven't you become the big Hollywood record producer type. This is Spider."

"Huh..." said Dallas.

"Damn, now where did he go?" I said looking into the crowd of exited passengers. "Must have made a dash for the restroom."

"Maybe he's still on the plane," said Dallas.

"What... No...," I stammered, "we were sitting at the very back."

"Carson, you alright?"

"What? Of course, I'm alright. Why in the hell wouldn't I be alright? Dude, don't look at me like that!"

"Maybe we should sit down," said Dallas, "you don't want to get too anxious."

"Hey, fuck you dude, I'm fine." I said starting to panic a little. "We'd better find the security station. They'll page h..."

"Carson, I've been standing here since the plane landed."

"So... So, what are you trying to say, Dallas? I know what you're thinking and you're dead wrong dude, I'm fine, I..."

"Brother, you walked through that ramp alone."

Chapter Four

Stratton Records Expands

It was a beautiful cliff-side house high up in the hills over Hollywood. Joey and his partner Dwayne had built it way back when Joey was still performing. Unimpressive from the exterior, the house presented little more than a three car garage with a front door and a tiny patch of shrubbery from the curb which was snug up against the building. Upon entering through the garage we were immediately exposed to why these were called cliff-side houses, the whole structure hung out over a cliff supported by exposed steel beams. The step down living room was huge, plate glass windows looked out over hills, houses, and then multi-colored lights for as far as the eye could see. Of course, I already knew the lay-out of the house; I'd been invited several times, still, looking down over the lower level and pool. Joey White had done very well by his young protégée upon his untimely death. Everything he owned or controlled came to Dallas Withers. And of course Skye was from a very wealthy family as well. This was a long, long way from Haight Street.

"So, you want to talk about it, man?" asked Dallas; coming poolside carrying a bottle and two long stem wine glasses.

"Dallas, don't," I said.

"You know we're always here for you, Carson."

"Yes I do know that," I said, "I love you guy's, man. When's Skye back in town? Okay, so just so you know I've already put in a call to Barnes."

"You still seeing that dude, damn, how longs it been now?"

"Hey, he got me out of the park, right?"

"I'm glad you're here, Carson," he said. "We're family, man. We should be spending more time."

"Barnes is taking me off the Prozac, you know that."

"And that's bad because?"

"Come on, Dallas," I said, "this is serious, man. I wasn't put on the shit because my life was so fuckin' wonderful."

"I know a guy here," said Dallas, "they tell me he's one of the best."

"Huh, you've got to be kidding me, dude! I would think that after all that happened, you of all people would be the very last dude to be recommending a fuckin' head doctor."

It had been about eighteen months. Eighteen long months of trying to make sense of all that had happened. It was Skye's mother, Colleen Prescott, a classic sociopath by most accounts; that had kicked off the evil fest. All totaled, six people wound up dead. Dallas, Skye and their housekeeper Etna came very close to being numbers seven through nine. As best I can recall the events of that wicked summer; Mrs. Prescott had put out a hit on Dallas after discovering not only was he continuing the long loathed homosexual relationship with her recently married son, but Ryan, his bride Heather and Dallas had concocted a scheme by which a child had been born. This baby, conceived of wife Heather and Dallas by artificial insemination, then adopted by her son, would along with his brother, born in the normal way, inherit the Howard Prescott fortune. Colleen had decided this would happen only over her dead body. Her detective/hit man failed his mission, and soon after Colleen Prescott landed herself on top of the hit list of a real killer.

It seemed the lights came on at the same moment the burgundy sheet slipped from my grasp.

"Good morning, Miss Etna," I said. "It seems like you get more beautiful every time I come to Los Angeles."

"Well, I sees yo eyesight done slip out on ya," she said. "Whatcha doin' here, Carson, yo daddy done run ya off again?"

"Naw, this is just a social visit," I said, "sorry, looks like I fell asleep out here again."

"I's reckon them two empty wine bottles played a part," she said. "Well you gotta pull it together, Carson, tired and sleepy or not. Dallas just called, got a car pickin' ya up in thirty five minutes."

"Huh, I just got here, what's he up to?"

"My guess, some fancy lunch place, told Etna don't feed ya nothin'."

"Well I sure hope nothing; doesn't include coffee."

"Ya still favor da Hazelnut and half & half I spose."

"Oh, bless you, Miss Etna," I said, "guess I'd better hop in the shower."

"First ya can drag all yo stuff in ta duh guess room like a normal person, Carson Elliot. Etna gettin' too old ta plays the bell hop."

"If I wasn't so poor I'd try to steal you away, Miss Etna," I said. "These two have got each other; I need you a lot more in San Francisco."

"Too cold, baby, sides des two needs ma help plenty; movin' back and foth like dey do. Now ya go on get yo' self cleaned up whilst I grind ya up some ma special coffee beans."

When I opened my suitcase there it was sitting right on top of the strapped in dress shirts, the novel. The very first I'd ever written, it was the copy that Spider... I picked it up, then sat on the bed rocking back and forth. What would I find when I opened it, would the yellow...

In a flash I flipped the book opened to about the middle page. There they were the highlighted lines, the lines I had sat quietly by and watched the Spider Man put there with my own eyes. 'Was I really losing it this time,' I wondered? 'Was it time for padded socks and bars on the windows?" After log moments of sitting there staring blankly at page 176 my memory and curiosity began to stir. I pondered, what was that whole scenario about? Whether real or some kind of delusion or day dream, surely there was some point in it. I remembered him or me or whatever the fuck; rambling on about writers being able to write more than... damn, what was it? I do remember this dude or whatever saying that if I could spend two years writing a four hundred page book of fictional prose and dialogue, it made no sense that I couldn't write a double spaced one or two page song. What kind of horse-shit thinking was that? As if writing lyrics had anything whatsoever to do with writing books. I flipped to page 1.

"Whatcha' doin' in dar, baby," yelled Etna, "don't hear no wadda runnin'. Well, ya best come on. I just hears da car pull up!"

I said nothing. After I'd pulled my lap-top from my carry-on I couldn't pull my eyes from the screen, keyboard, or the book. When she came back to the locked guest room door the second time, this time knocking, I yelled, "I'm not feeling well, Etna! Tell the driver for me please, I'm not coming!"

"What...Carson Elliot, ya open dis here door!"

"Not now, Etna," I said, "I'll explain later, honey!" I did not want to lose my concentration. "And would you call Dallas for me! Please, Miss Etna; I'll be out in a bit!"

"Well..."

"Thanks honey." I said going hungrily back to work. I looked back over the words I had written some ten years earlier as if with new eyes. The muse was right. There was beautiful music playing between the lines.

"I can't believe it," said Dallas; putting the finished pages down on the coffee table. "My God, man, we've known you over ten years. Since before the beginning of all this. Why in the hell wouldn't you have said…"

"Well, is it any good, man?" I asked. "Be honest with me, Dallas."

"Are you kidding me," he said, "this is a whole lot better than good! Dude, you wrote five songs since I saw you last night. I just don't understand, why in all these years…"

"Dallas, focus up. Are these real songs?"

"You've got to let me fax them to Skye."

"So, you like them," I said? "It seems like you do, but…"

"Dude, these are some of the most beautiful lyrics I've ever read," said Dallas, "welcome to Stratton Records, my friend."

"Who said I was pitching for a job? That's not why I came here man, I…"

"Well, go on," he said, "you came here to…"

"Fuck you! You know damn well why I came here."

"Carson, come on, let's not go back down that rabbit hole. Point is you're here now."

"So, just hypothetically speaking," I said, "how would it work?"

"The music?"

"No, the snowmobiling. Come on, Dallas, these are just words, right, may as well say poems."

"Well, I'm just the singer in this family," he said, "you're going to have to work with Skye. Man, this is going to blow him away, dude. Who would have thought that you of all people."

"It's writing," I said shrugging my shoulders, "I'm a writer."

"You've always been a writer, what's with the sudden interest in music, gospel music at that?"

"Well, I don't know that it's totally sudden."

"Come on, Carson," he said "how long we known each other, man? Why now?"

"You really want me to... I thought you didn't like the rabbit hole."

"I love the lyrics, dude, just caught me a little off guard. The company needs this, man. We can't or at least shouldn't expect Skye to be writing for three different artists. He's way past exhausted, and with everything that's been going on in Manhattan."

"It's about to start?"

"We're thinking maybe we should bring Heather and the boys here until it's over," said Dallas. "The Prescott's still own that apartment in Paris, but we can't do that to them again, man. We can't do that to ourselves again."

"Cody and Dean, how old are they now?"

"Almost three and five," said Dallas, "my God man..." he wiped his eyes with the palm of his hand.

I walked over to embrace my old friend. We sat there on a corner of their living room sofa, he wept just a little and we held each other tight.

As a company limousine pulled into a heavy steel electronic gate at the side of the old Uptown Theater in the heart of downtown Los Angeles, it seemed, at least to me, that Stratton Records had swollen to twice its size since my last visit. Of course, nothing had actually changed at all. At least not to the exterior of the building, taking a snap-shot from directly in front of the structure you could easily be standing in 1929. What was different was the way I was seeing the company.

"Skye's, up on skype," said Dallas's personal assistant, Gloria, peeking into his office. The two of us had come into his office very early; or at least it was early for me. Even since I had gone back to work for my parents I rarely got up before noon. Skye had been faxed eleven pages of lyrics and notes the night before.

"My old buddy," said Skye through the computer, "how are you, citizen?"

This of course had been the way he had addressed me on our initial meeting in Golden Gate Park so long ago. As far as I knew Dallas had not yet told him about my 'episode'. I'd asked him not to. Skye had much too much going on in Manhattan to be worrying about me and my fragile mind coming apart once again in sunny California. I didn't think it right to be asking him about stupid song lyrics or any other work at a time like this. But after a couple hours of us going back and forth Dallas convinced me that his partner in work and love would greatly appreciate some sort of distraction.

"Hey, babe," said Dallas over my shoulder, "I miss you."

"It's only been two hours," said Skye. "Look we've got to talk fast; got a hearing in about an hour. Carson, so I'm sure you've already heard that I'm wild about the lyrics. There'll be no problem at all with the music, in fact I've already got some great ideas."

"Just like I said, right," said Dallas squeezing my shoulder a little, "I don't think the dude really believed me," he said into the monitor.

"We'll make it work, if that's what you really want Carson," said Skye. "I mean if a couple records is all you really want."

"Huh," said Dallas, "of course that's what he wants. That's what we do here Skye... have you had any sleep?"

"Actually, not a whole lot," said Skye, "spent most of the night re-reading an old novel I downloaded. A very interesting story, I identified so much with the characters."

"They're my words, man," I said, "I wrote them; I wrote every single..."

"Carson Elliot, I've got one word for you," said Skye, "ready?"

"Skye, I've got every right to...," I said!

"Musical," said Skye. "Look, it's a great story, Carson. Why break it up? Dude, I know how you feel about your work, and I know how hard it's been trying to interest readers. I say we do "A Perfect Place to Hide," as a gospel musical."

"A musical," yelled Dallas from behind me! "Skye, exactly what in the hell do we know about..."

"Chalk it up to having more than enough money in our coffers, man," said Skye. "We can well afford to experiment, maybe expand a little. I'm thinking, turn the focus from the crime to the redemption, and of course the lives of the kids living in the park. Lord knows there's enough talent between the three of us and Stratton Records. What we don't know we'll learn and what we can't do on our own, well that's where money comes in handy.

Look, you guys, I'm from New York, I know a few people in theater."

"You're serious?" I asked staring directly into the web cam.

"As serious as a man whose father is about to go on trial for four counts of first degree murder," said Skye. "Okay, so I've got to get over to the courthouse, guys. Carson, download a few books on both playwriting and adapting a novel for stage. Let's figure out who we need to get on board. We'll talk more in the morning."

"I love you, Skye," said Dallas. "I pray it goes well today, babe."

"We'll both be praying," I said.

"Hello, Mr. Elliot," said Dr. Randal Epstein after I'd been shown into his office. "Please, please, come in, sit, sit."

"Thank you for seeing me, Dr. Epstein," I said taking the man's hand for two quick shakes before taking a seat on one of his two burgundy tufted leather sofas. He sat on the other sofa directly in front of me. This man was old. He looked to me like how I would imagine Sigmund Freud would have looked in his last days of practice. The Beverly Hills office on Wilshire Boulevard was very nice, much nicer than I could even come close to affording. What was Dallas thinking sending me to a place like this? All I needed was a quick switch-up on my anti-depressant. This was far from the first time. But he had insisted, which I found pretty amazing since it was Joey White's psychiatrist, a Dr. Kenneth Tully, from San Francisco who came very close to putting him, Skye and Etna to everlasting sleep. Yes, there were two murderous scenarios played out almost simultaneously that wicked summer of blood. Thankfully the murderous doctor here on the west coast was not nearly as efficient or successful as Skye's father in the east. Though it was not proven, the cops and close to everyone involved in the case felt certain that very same doctor had murdered Joey. I did not want to be there, but I also didn't want to be walking around seeing and talking to people who... anyway I needed off the Prozac, and I needed this dude to put some kind of new Band-Aid on my brain so I wouldn't fuck this up. The way Skye had been talking I might be on the verge of actually seeing some movement in my dismal career. Though I thought it a little strange to see myself going from novelist to songwriter, a novelist adapting his own work for the stage seemed by comparison almost cliché. Throw in the opportunity to bring my first book, the beloved yet virtually ignored, first born son to the stage.

"So, shall we get right to it then," said Dr. Epstein? "You've come here because you want me to give you drugs, yes?"

"I wouldn't put it quite like..."

"I'm only going by what you said to my new secretary over the telephone," he said. "Mrs. Shelby, a nice woman, I don't know her well. Let me see..." he continued while looking over a spiral note pad. "Yes, yes, you told this nice woman that it was urgent that you see me; that you wanted to be taken off one drug and put on another, and that money was no object, yes?"

"I'm sorry. I was probably a little manic. Sincerely, I'm sorry doctor I... "

"Okay, so we understand this woman is a secretary? Tell me how I can help you young man, and please, let's not begin with talk of prescriptions. For that you can go to any clinic or hospital, yes?"

"You're not one for mixing words."

"Yes, yes, that is correct," said Dr. Epstein, "your time is valuable. So now tell me, what's going on with you lately?"

"Sure, I can start there if you want," I said, "but my problems go back long before this current situation."

"You're a young man."

"I was put on Ritalin at eleven years old," I said, "that was only the beginning."

"Already back with the prescriptions," said Dr. Epstein. "Listen we'll get there soon enough. If we want to reach some destination; make some sort of progress, you'll agree to let me drive, yes?"

This guy was making me nuts with the yes, yes, and yeses. But somehow I kinda liked him, more to the point I felt like I could trust him. This was a strictly no bullshit kinda guy. At this point in my life the very last thing I needed was another lazy ass, pill pushing bullshit specialist of a psychiatrist. "Okay, so a few weeks back I started noticing this guy, a very talented, extremely good looking guy, hanging out and making music in a subway concourse in San Francisco."

"You use the term, "extremely good looking" to describe this man. You are homosexual?"

"Yes I am, is that going to be a..."

"Let's not waste your time with these kinds of questions. I am a doctor. May I call you, Carson?"

"Sure, and I'll call you…"

"Doctor is fine. So, this man catches your attention. Please, go on."

"Actually I noticed his voice first," I said, "such a beautiful, perfectly pitched…"

"How long before the face?"

"Huh? Well, I guess I must have seen what he looked like. I mean the sound wasn't coming over the intercom. Anyway, I'd just hear him singing and playing on a somewhat beat up old battery operated keyboard pretty much every morning as I passed through the station. After a couple weeks an idea started percolating. You see I know these two guys, actually they're good friends. I'm visiting them here in LA now. Anyway my friends are record producers, and I thought maybe they could help this kid."

"Why were you there?"

"Huh?"

"This place, the subway concourse," said Dr. Epstein peering over his glasses, "You said you passed through this place every morning. Why, this is where you work, live?"

"Actually, I was unemployed at that time," I said. "I'm a writer doctor, a novelist. There's a coffee shop at that stop where I sometimes go to write."

"But you said you would see the young man playing there every morning."

"Alright, so I was hanging out there a lot more around the time I started noticing this guy. It's a Starbucks in the heart of downtown San Francisco, there are copious samplings of humanity moving back and forth... look I was trying to flesh out new characters for a book, that's it."

"And did you?"

"Did I what?"

"You say you were there every morning to find inspiration for new characters," said Dr. Epstein. "I'm asking if you were successful."

"Not really," I said, "I guess the real answer would be, no. In fact I ended up deleting three quarters of what I already had. I haven't touched the project in weeks."

"This person under the ground, this singer, you wanted to fuck him, yes?"

"No! No," I said, "I just wanted to help him. My friends, they could..."

"Why?"

"Huh?"

"Why help him," asked Dr. Epstein. "You haven't said anything that would indicate this man was asking for your help. You're not in the music business. I've been to San Francisco and all the downtown stations many times over the years. Those guys, the ones who play the instruments, they're generally expecting what, a dollar, two dollars, something like that, yes?"

"Do you always end every sentence with, yes?"

"Yes, yes. I use this word a lot. It's not the worst crime, no?" he laughed. "Okay, so let's concede at least for the moment that you had no physical attraction to this person. Help me to understand his importance.

"Great to see you again, man," said Skye passing me a plate of fresh banana waffles. "You look good, Carson. Still hard to believe you and my honey man are not related."

"Can't rule it totally out," said Dallas going for the bacon, "your folks spend any time in Texas, my man."

Skye had come in on a late flight long after I had once again fallen asleep on their living room sofa. There was just something about that sofa and me. I had awakened to the aroma

of Etna's mouthwatering banana waffles and bacon strips.

"So, how's your dad, Skye," I asked.

"He's off suicide watch again," said Skye, "but, well, you can

imagine."

"With all due respect, babe," said Dallas, "there is no death

penalty in New York State. What do the attorneys hope to

accomplish with all these delays?"

"Everybody deserves the best trial they can afford," said

Skye. "Look, we all know my dad will never breathe free air again,

the question is not that he will be given at least one life sentence.

At this point it's all about where he'll do the time. Fuck, man, he's

not a monster, two of the deaths were accidents. The State is not

even disputing that. He feels horrible about... I'm sorry guy's..." he

trailed off. "Okay, now really, no more of that today. The man is

off suicide watch and in protective custody. Let's talk about

what's going on here and now."

"I met with a, Dr. Epstein," I said. "He's kind of a strange old guy."

"Carson…" said Dallas, "I told you I wasn't going to say anything about…"

"Epstein, the shrink," said Skye, "you okay, man?"

"All things being relative," I said. "No crazier than usual. Well maybe that's not really true."

"Come on, you guys," said Dallas shooting me a let's not go there look, "half the people we know see therapists or psychiatrists or witch doctors, somethin'. It's the LA way."

"Anything you want to talk about, Carson," asked Skye. "I mean I totally get that it's personal, but if you want to talk about anything."

"Naw, I'm cool."

"Well, strange and funny looking or not, Epstein is the best," said Skye. "There's a very receptive mind and even a decent sense of humor behind all those wrinkles."

"You mean you've seen…" I started.

"Anyway," said Dallas, "this is going to be great, man, the three of us working together. So what's the plan?"

I knew Dallas felt he was protecting me by continually moving the conversation away from psychiatry and I was actually kinda glad he did, I was not up for yet another session of skeptical awkward silences, sideways stares or watching these guys gaze fall to their shoelaces. I had been the center of that particular kind of attention far too often in my youth, these where neither pleasant nor welcome memories. By the time I reached adolescence my fanciful stories had become my 'creative imagination,' enhanced no doubt by my 'medications.' To many of my teachers and my aunt Gert I was simply a liar. In my own mind, a storyteller, yes I'll admit that way back then I was well aware of my bending and manipulating small fragments of truth into big, bold fanciful tales. Anyway, I knew early on that I intended to write fiction someday. For me the daily challenge was to get anyone I could get to listen to me to believe whatever I told them was the truth. However this is not at all what was going on right now. No this thing with the Spider Man, this was no game.

Chapter Five

The Amazing Spider Man

"Hey, could you pull over?" I asked leaning up to the Stratton driver, Henry. "Better yet, make a U-turn here, Henry."

"Mr. Elliot, I can't...!"

"Come on man, take it back to that corner," I yelled, "or let me out... never mind." I was out of the car. Suddenly I found myself standing in the center of Sunset Boulevard; amidst blaring car horns, pumping breaks, and a chorus of, "get the fuck out of the street, asshole!" I had to move quickly, I crossed to the curb going in the opposite direction. As luck would have it there was a city bus pulling up to that very spot. Now the other kind of luck; no fuckin' change, I slipped a twenty into the slot and grabbed one of the aisle facing old people seats. Two stops up I was off the bus again. This is the spot where I had seen him, *'how far I wondered could he have moved on foot; that is assuming of course that he was still on foot.'* I quickly crossed the many lanes that separated the Sunset Strip. The old Tower Records building sat on the North-West corner of the intersection and directly behind the place where I was damn near positive I had just seen Spider. I peeked into maybe six businesses around the intersection, nothing. When Henry pulled the limo over to a curb just in front of me, I waved him off with a circle the block signal, on the second time around I got in the car. It was over, I'd lost him.

"You want me to cruise around a little," asked Henry. "Maybe they took off in the other direction."

"Naw, it's cool," I said, "just thought I saw an old friend. Hey, you think we could just keep this to our... There he is, pull over...!"

"The doctor will see you now, Mr. Elliot," said Mrs. Shelby buzzing the inner office door.

"Yes, please, sit, sit," said Dr. Epstein. "So tell me, how are you, Carson?"

"Something happened yesterday," I said. "Not a good day, not even close."

"Okay?"

"Actually, it's not okay. So there's a reason I'm still on this shit right?"

"What's happened, Carson?"

"Maybe nothing... ," I said. "Look, I spent a couple hours yesterday chasing a ghost. I don't know doctor; I could have sworn I saw him two; maybe three times."

"This man from under the street?"

"He told me to call him, Spider."

"You spoke with this person," asked Dr. Epstein, "there was interaction?"

"No not yesterday. Okay, so like I was saying last week, I met this homeless dude in San Francisco, he told me then he went by the name, Spider. I gave him a job, he moved into the basement of my apartment building. I thought you wrote some of this down."

"I remember what was said. I wrote in my notes that you came here because you felt like you were having delusions; most likely brought on by the high dose of Prozac you've been taking for several months. So this is not accurate, you're not convinced this person was and/or is a delusion?"

"You're the doctor."

"Yes, yes, this is true," he said, "tell me more about this person. We'll come back to yesterday's incidents."

"Like what?"

"Anything you can remember. This name is obviously not his real name."

"It never came up, that's how he introduced himself. Is that important?"

"We can't run a check on a guy named, Spider. Go on, please."

"He said he was from Fresno," I said. "I don't know, he's bi-racial, Black and Jewish I think...yeah, his mom is Jewish. Something about his father being in prison. We never got into why. Look doctor, I knew this guy for less than three weeks."

"And as far as you know, you're the only person who's actually seen this person?"

"It's very confusing talking about him. It's almost like trying to remember the details of a dream."

"Let's talk about yesterday," he said. "You saw this person, yes?"

"Yes, on Sunset Boulevard, at about Larrabee. I was being driven to meet my friends for lunch... you know I'm not clear about something. My friend Dallas is who recommended you, yet it's his partner who seems to know you."

"You said you've seen doctors, therapists. You understand confidentiality. Let's not be distracted, this driver of the car, a taxi?"

"No, my friends have a company car drive me around. I don't drive."

"The driver didn't see him?"

"I shouldn't cut back on my own," I said, "at least not with some kind of back-up plan. I've had a few bad experiences."

"Cut back to half your usual dose," said Epstein, "we'll come back to this next visit."

We were sitting in Skye's office at Stratton Records. I had

decided to resist the urge to ask him if he had been a patient of

Epstein's. The good doctor was right of course. The man had

every right to his privacy. Besides if he wanted me to know. Of

course he would have to have been seeing somebody. My friend,

Skye, had, had one hell of a couple years.

"Okay, so we understand what we're up against here," said

Dallas. "We need to squeeze this whole story into about seventy-

five minutes on stage; ninety would be the absolute top. Can this

even be done?"

"I've got more pages," I said, "but I've got to tell you guy's I

don't know a damn thing about what I'm supposed to be doing

here. I've only even seen one gospel musical in my life. I think we

should at least consider getting a playwright."

"What's to adapt," said Skye, "it's a musical, man. Look, we

want your name all over this thing, Carson. This is your baby, man.

I don't know if you're aware of this, but you've damn near written a Broadway musical already, dude. Remember we're talking about seventy-five minutes, brother. We've got more than enough words; it's all about setting it to music now."

"I'll set up some meetings with choreographers and set designers," said Dallas, "in fact, I've already spoken with a couple agents."

"How are you going to choreograph words, Dallas," I asked? "So, we're all in agreement about ditching the crime and criminals altogether?"

"Yeah, I'm sorry, man," said Skye. "But the material still works as is, Carson, just a bit of tweaking most of which can be done by Skype. Instead of a physical park "A Perfect Place to Hide," becomes a spiritual place, the park only as metaphor. Okay, so I guess the ball is in my court now, let's meet up again in a couple weeks, see what we have."

"Okay, so you both agree to play yourselves for at least the California run?" I asked rhetorically. This had been the main condition from the very start. "I've got to get back to the city, the Republican is about to shit a brick."

"Why does it always have to be, "The City," said Dallas, "What the hell is LA supposed to be?"

"Me-tro-po-lis," said Skye and me in unison.

"Mind if I sit here?"

"Oh, my God! My God," I said, "Spider."

"Is that a yes," he asked taking the seat next to me. The passengers and luggage had been loaded, the boarding ramp secured. This wasn't a good time for screaming.

"Dude, what the fuck? I don't understand, what the hell is going on?!"

"Of course not," he said, "so have you missed me?"

I slammed my head hard against the back of the seat in front of me, then again and then... "Did I miss you? Dude, are you out of you're motha' fuckin' mind?!"

"Don't do that again, Carson," said the Spider Man, "save the high drama for your novels. I'm proud of you."

"Am I having some kind of episode, psychotic break, or whatever the fuck?"

"What difference does it really make, man? Point is I'm here, we're able to communicate, relax a little, it is, what it is."

"And what exactly the fuck is that," I asked? "Hey, why is it that I get the feeling nobody on this plane can hear us?"

"Are you really on an airplane right now? Maybe you're asleep. That would probably be the best bet. Maybe you were dreaming the whole time we were together from the start. At least that would mean you weren't "cray, cray." I just don't think it makes much difference dude. It's good to see you again. You did good."

"Okay, so what the hell. I guess you're right, dreaming, that would certainly explain a lot. Alright so I'm dreaming, so how does it work?"

"I'm here, just accept it," he said. "Anyway like I was saying, I'm very proud of you, Carson. You said on the first day that my voice inspired you, looks like you were right."

"I'm still not quite there, or here or where ever the fuck. Keep talking."

"You wanted inspiration," he said, "desperate for an idea that would work, shake you out of your rut. You even started praying again. By the way that was a very good decision."

"You're really not from Fresno are you?"

"No."

"The family," I asked, "the father in prison?"

"Details, details," he said. "Well, we can spend this time discussing me if you want. I'd much rather spend whatever time we have discussing us and going forward with our work."

"What us," I said! "You said you weren't even gay."

He laughed at this. "I'm not straight either. What is the relationship between an artist and his muse? I seriously doubt its anything physical, Carson."

"You just lost me kid," I said. "So you are literally my muse, that it?"

"You think of me as being very beautiful don't you," he said. "Want to take a guess why?"

"You're okay, I don't know about beautiful. Okay, so if I dreamed you up, I guess it would make sense that you'd fit my idea of something perfect."

"You've got a very vivid imagination, my friend," said Spider. "So of course I'm the most beautiful creature..."

"Okay, enough of that," I said. "So, if you are my inspiration, muse if you like, shouldn't you be…"

"Yeah, I should be inspiring you. We're going to have to help each other, Carson."

"Huh?"

"There's something trying to kill me," he said. "Only you have the power to keep me alive, my friend."

"What?"

"This project is in good hands," he said. "You've got to get back to writing. Get back into the new novel, the book you were writing when we met."

"Dude, this is far from over," I said, "I've got to walk this project all the way to the stage, what's the matter with you, Spider. I thought this is what you wanted."

"When you stop writing," he said, "I will surely die. The adversary will win. In your heart you love me. Write Carson. Keep me alive, I want to be with you."

"Sir, sir," it was a stewardess. "I'm sorry sir but I'm going to have to ask you to fasten your seat belt as we prepare for landing.

"What the hell is going on," I screamed into the ear under the helmet of the man blocking my way! "What's happened?"

"Fire sir," yelled the fireman over his shoulder! I noticed three stripes on his sleeve. "I'm going to have to ask you to step back behind the cones, sir."

"That's my damn building, mister!" I yelled, "Who's in charge here!"

"You're the owner," he asked?

"My parents own the building, I'm the manager. I also live here!"

"The good news is; the fire was contained to only two apartments at the rear of the building."

"And the bad," I asked already having a pretty good idea based on the only remnants of smoke I could see.

"Bum luck, most likely electrical," he said, "90% probability it started in the manager's unit, sir."

"How in the hell could you cause an electrical fire when you've been fuckin' AWOL for the last two weeks," yelled the Republican! "For Christ sakes, Carson, you realize they'll be knocking holes in plaster all through the fucking building now!"

"We've been passing inspections," I yelled back at him. "Damn, shouldn't we be at least a little grateful no one was hurt! Or maybe you would have preferred I'd been asleep in that bed!"

"That's enough," yelled my mother, "what an awful thing to say, Carson Elliot! I think you should apologize to your father."

"Well, I don't agree with you, mother," I said. "He probably would just as soon be done with me and all my waste and embarrassment. Look at the bright side of all this dad, maybe now you'll get some of that wasted tuition money back from the insurance company."

"Get the fuck out of my house!" screamed the Republican, "I mean it, boy, get out!"

"Burned out remember," I yelled back. "You just try throwing me out on the street! Go ahead, I dare you!"

"Don't tempt me, boy," he said. "You're right about one thing; my life would be a whole lot easier to live without you in it!"

"Marshall," yelled my mother! "How could you say something like that?"

"Don't stop him, mother," I said, "let the man tell his truth. Then I'll tell both of you mine."

She turned on her heel; dramatically flipping her very good weave down and then up over her face. The two story penthouse apartment was huge; thankfully my reserve bedroom was on the first floor and opposite end of the apartment; I could be there weeks without ever encountering them. The Republican started to say something then thought better of it and made his way to his study and no doubt a few fingers of Scotch without another word. These two definitely worked better as a team. Oh well, at least I still had my luggage which of course contained my computer and all my work.

As I lay there in the bed of my childhood unable to sleep, unable to stop thinking of him my mind drifted back over that last conversation. What was he talking about? Something was trying to kill him, only I could keep him alive. What I found so disturbing about this whole Spider Man thing was why in the hell I could

remember so much. Never in all my life, not even considering all

the psychotropic medications I'd taken throughout the years of

my discontent had I been able to remember even a bit. An idea

popped into my head... I was out of the bed. In the closet I found

it there on the floor, my trunk. Though this room here in the

Oakland high-rise had never actually been my bedroom my

parents kept everything I'd never claimed stored here. Before I

opened the latch I knew exactly what I would find, and I was right.

There it was filling the bottom half of the trunk; the entire

collection.

This little epiphany was so simple and obvious it made me

sad enough to cry. Any normal person would have put this

together on the first day. Certainly it shouldn't have taken more

than a week. But I had known for years that I'd retained no

childhood memories before eight maybe nine years old. Now

before me lay the physical evidence. As a very little boy I had been

obsessed with 'The Amazing Spiderman," this was the super hero
that I knew would someday come to save me.

"But you have a doctor there in San Francisco," said Dr.
Epstein over the phone, "yes, yes, a, Dr. Barnes. You've seen him
for several years, yes?"

"Barnes, is out," I said, "I've been seeing him far too long
and with no real results. I mean shouldn't he have put this
superhero, cartoon, whatever the fuck thing together long before
now."

"It's only a name," said Epstein, "yes? You could just as
easily have collected Batman or The Green Hornet. If the person
were called by another name, what would it matter? Still, this
character having a root in your subconscious is significant,
perhaps Dr. Barnes..."

"Look, I'm not seeing, Barnes, again," I said. "There was another incident on the plane. I took your advice, about sleeping with the pad and pen I mean, I got a lot down."

"Excellent," he said, "now the very moment you hang up have them faxed to me here at my office, yes, yes, this is very important."

"What about the fire, Epstein," I asked? "As far as I know dreams don't set real live fires."

"Any chance it was just an accident as was reported in The Chronicle?"

"I didn't leave an iron on, Doctor," I said. "And even if I did and the automatic cut off was somehow defective, two weeks is one hell of a delay don't you think?"

"Yes, yes," he said, "we'll have to wait for the report. But bring a copy of the receipt from your taxi ride, yes?"

"I didn't set it," I yelled. "Why would I burn my own fucking apartment? People live there for Christ sakes; do you realize how easily people could have been killed? Fuck!"

"Okay, so I have patients waiting, yes," he said. "I don't want you taking any more Prozac. According to your file you are familiar with Xanax, yes?"

"I'm worried," said Dallas after hearing of the event's, "are you alright, Carson, are you safe?"

"I just wish I had a clearer head that's all," I said. "I just spoke with Epstein. He's switching me to Xanax."

"Are more drugs really the only answer?"

"Well, you sure hit the nail on the head there," I said. "I'm not taking it man. In fact I'm not even filling the scrip."

"I'm not a doctor, Carson," he said, "and neither are you. When are you coming back to LA?"

"Well, technically I'm homeless," I said, "nether of the parents know what to say about all this. All we do is argue."

"They know about, Spider?"

"Dallas, let's not call him that anymore," I said. "Look, I really would like to get out of here, out of this city I mean."

"Sure, you know you're welcome here, man," said Dallas. "What about the cops, the fire department?"

"I'm free to leave. The insurance company probably won't like it but so what. I didn't burn up my own place, man, it's not like I'll be collecting anything. I don't own shit Dallas, and now I don't even have personal crap. Good thing I had my toothbrush, shaver and laptop with me."

"Don't worry about Epstein or anything else, brother," he said, "I got you covered. Gloria will arrange the flight ASAP."

"You're a good dude, and a great friend, Dallas," I said, "I won't forget this. You're sure it will be cool with Skye?"

"What do you think? I gotta warn you though, the man's a workaholic. Don't count on getting a lot of sleep."

"Oh fuck, the play," I said. "Well, I guess if Skye can still work with all he's had to deal with."

Timothy Blaine

Chapter Six

The Work

Skye began the session with a few chords from what he hoped would be the opening and theme. Dallas came in at exactly six minutes with the lyrics to "Will You Be My Friend?" and then merged it with a fast paced number I written called, "We've Done Something Bad." Though I had intended the "bad" song for much later in the play, it worked a lot better the way they put it together. After a duet ballad sung acapella by Dallas and a young blonde actress already cast for the female lead, we broke for comments and brainstorming.

"I think this is a hell of a start," I said trying very hard to maintain focus. I don't know how these guys did it. I mean images and video footage of Skye's parent's previous lives together and non-stop media coverage of the trial had to be the talk of the country, not to mention France, considering Skye's family's dual citizenship. How could we just walk into a studio? Skye's been wearing a ratty brown wig and fake goatee around LA. Even though the Stratton Limo's back windows were darkly tinted and pulled directly into the very secure company lot, the situation at the Hollywood house was much more tenuous. After the tragic and heavily covered crimes on both coasts just eighteen months past, keeping Ryan Prescott's California identity separate and private had all but been impossible.

"Okay so with just an intro and three songs we've established the basic story line," said Skye. "This is good. What do you think, Dallas?"

"The ballad is weak," said Dallas, "I'm not feeling it at all. The acapella thing is just not working for me. It's too long and trying to carry way too much information."

"Okay," said Skye, "Carson?"

"He's got a point," I said, "it could be shorter, maybe even cut in half. Seems like we need to build a lot more momentum, you know get a rhythm, a beat."

"What about the rest of it," asked Skye; whom it was decided would also direct the play? "We need to get something for choreography."

"I'd say yeah, up to that piece," said Dallas, "I really think you guy's should at least consider scrapping it all together."

"Damn," I said, "that bad, huh?"

"I'm feeling kinda strongly about it, Carson," said Dallas, "just doesn't work for me, man. Can't we just stick to musical storytelling and a little dialogue?"

"Take it easy," said Skye. "After we break for the day,

Carson and I will see if any part of the damn thing can be used."

"Skye, you've got to get some rest, babe," said Dallas. "You

can't keep up this pace, man."

"Dallas, I'm flying out late tomorrow night," said Skye, "I

need to leave you guy's with something to work with. Maybe we

should just table the song and scene for the moment. Come on,

there are another two songs to get through and that, my friends

will be happening before we break."

I don't know how she did it. Etna Jackson had to be

seventy-five years old. I know for a fact Joey White had provided

for her in his will. Plus she had her own house and plenty of family

to look after her back in Alabama. She'd worked for Joey and his

partner only a short time before Dwayne was gunned down by an

obsessed or possessed teenager. Then nursed and micromanaged

the life of the clinically depressed survivor several years only to be present as his life was taken as well while she lay asleep a few yards away. And then to have her own life nearly taken along with Skye and Dallas's by that mad doctor.

"Good morning Miss Etna," I said walking into the kitchen, "Dallas here?"

"He be up in a minute," she said, "what'cha' like ta eat dis mornin' baby? Etna don't make waffles ever' mornin'"

"Well, the main thing is coffee of course. Sausage Biscuit, if you have it."

"Wit' orange juice and a little bowl of ma special grits," she said, "Comin' right up."

"Etna, still pushing grits I see," said Dallas coming into the room, "same here honey. A little cheese on my biscuit, please."

"Course," she said.

"How'd you sleep," I asked.

"Took one of Skye's Ambien," said Dallas, "I was out before he left the house."

"I don't know how you guys do it, man," I said. "Are you ever together?"

"It's just this fuckin' trial, man. He really wants to be there for his Dad. I mean he actually has a lot of empathy for the guy. Colleen was not a very nice person. Actually she was the worst! Controlling, domineering, greedy, narcissistic, bitter... she tried to have me killed, dude!"

"You never go back with him," I asked.

"Oh, I have done and will be doing plenty more day trips," he said. "It's just, for the trial... you know. Prosecutors are going to make this plenty ugly. We can count on that."

"Heather and the kids, what's it like for them, Dallas?"

"Heather's there in court with him for every hearing," he said. "I'm really hoping Skye can talk her into letting the boys come here for a while, even if it means renting something away from this place."

"I noticed all the house phones are unplugged," I said.

"Thank God the media hounds can only get as close as the bottom of the hill," said Dallas. "Cops and security patrol won't allow stopping on the single lane up here. Man, I can't even begin to express how grateful I am that you're here right now Carson. That goes for Skye as well. I think all three of us could use a good friend right about now."

"You think they'll actually be hearing the case soon, Dallas," I asked?

"I wish," he said, "this is all still preliminary shit man. We're looking at least another year, maybe two. Anyway, even without the trial and all its accompanying drama, Skye spends a lot of time in Manhattan. He wants the boys to grow up with at least one full time dad."

"How does it work, man," I asked? "I mean you're Cody's biological father."

"Heather is a great woman. Let's be clear there," he said. "I mean, can you imagine? To be honest, we're no closer to figuring out how to work this family dynamic than we were on the day little Cody was conceived."

"They're going to stay married?"

"Can you believe this whole thing started over fuckin' money," said Dallas? "Yeah, let's just go ahead and call the damn thing out, man. The only reason Skye married Heather was because his fuckin' grandfather had stipulated that he be married and father a male heir to inherit all his fuckin' money."

"That was Dean," I said. "That's sort of the way rich people think, Dallas, especially, old school, straight, white, rich people. But you guys went on, strategically planning Cody's birth."

"Cody makes us family," he said. "He's a child born to all three of us. Look, man we love both of our kids, in my heart Skye is my husband as I am his. It's just that…"

"Heather."

"Yeah, well, it's just not right, man," said Dallas. "Heather is a beautiful woman; with a big heart, a perfect mother. She deserves to have her own husband, a real husband; you know."

"And you," I asked, "what about you, and Skye too for that matter?"

"It won't be long before the boys start asking questions," he said. "That part we could probably handle under our version of 'normal' conditions. It's not like tens of thousands of gay and lesbian parents don't go through the same thing. It's just all this fuckin' publicity man! Reporters can be like animals when they're in competition. No doubt the Prescott fortune, the will, the marriage, everything's coming out. Even if we can manage to shield the kids from this for the time being, it'll all be public record, Carson."

"Damn, those poor boys."

"Let's at least be grateful that it's all happening now," he said, "while they're so young. School is still years away, I just hope that, that... Fuck, Carson, we can't allow Cody to go through life thinking this whole thing was brought on by his birth man! That fucking witch, I wish she could have been killed more than once! Fuck, what kind of a sick fuckin' mind!"

"I'm falling in love with you," I said. "Does that even make sense, Muse?"

"More will be revealed," he said. "Don't overthink it, Carson. Something important is happening here. So you've changed my name?"

"I feel like a damn fool," I said, "I mean, com'on, man, fuckin' cartoons! Okay, so you're not a real person, still... *'I just told a make believe person that I'm falling in love with him.'*

"It's something that needs to happen."

"What? What the hell does that mean, what needs to happen?"

"You need to love me, Carson Elliot," he said, "it's the only way we'll survive. There is an adversary; she doesn't like me very much."

"She?"

"She's been with you a long time, my friend," he said. "Not a good person, but make no mistake, Carson, she is a person, or at least; a personality."

"What, dude what the fuck are you talking about? Who the fuck!? What, a woman?"

"I'm upsetting you."

"I just don't understand why you talk in riddles," I said, "what woman? I hardly know any women. And by the way, don't think for a moment I'm not aware that you're totally side stepping what I just said to you."

"Come again."

"Just an old human custom," I said. "Generally speaking when someone tells you they love you they're hoping for... *'Fuck, what the hell am I talking about?'*

"What do you know about love, Carson?"

"Why are you doing this to me, man?"

"Man?"

"Okay, that's it. You can go now."

"Can I?"

"Fuck you, asshole! Leave me the fuck alone!"

"You told me once you loved my vocals," he said. "Let me sing for you now Carson."

"Whatever, dude."

I could hear music, instruments playing in my head. It wasn't a new song. I'd heard it before. I'd always liked it; a Frampton classic. My muse sang for me in that angelic voice that had caught my attention under the streets of San Francisco, "I'm in You."

"So it sounds like most of what you've been experiencing could be explained by sleep or a kind of daydreaming, yes," said Dr. Epstein.

"No," I said, "I wasn't asleep for that bullshit in the limo a couple weeks back. And I wasn't asleep yesterday."

"But you were alone, yes?"

"I don't know, man," I said, "one minute I'm listening to him sing a seventies love song, next thing I remember is Miss Etna coming through the garage door carrying groceries."

"So you were alone in the house," said Epstein, "we can rule out neither sleep nor daydreaming."

"Are we going somewhere with this, doctor? I thought we were past this point. I've already accepted that this dude lives only in my head. Maybe you can help me understand why he's still hanging around? I've been off the Prozac for weeks."

"This was your diagnosis," he said, "an assumption you made before coming to me. So, now only the Xanax, yes?"

"No, I didn't fill the prescription." I said, "Look, I don't want any more drugs doctor, this is the clearest my head has been in years. I can't ask my friends to keep paying for these sessions indefinitely. Maybe we should get to the things I wrote down after my little visit yesterday."

"Sure, but we must come back to this issue, yes."

"Okay, so Miss Etna distracted me for a bit. Maybe fifteen, twenty minutes later, I wrote this down," I said handing him the little note book he'd instructed me to carry around. "The notes are lousy I know. Something about a woman. A woman wants to kill him, something like that."

"The word love is here as well, and this song," he said. "A good song. This is different."

"He was singing when I first became aware of him."

"Only gospel music," he said, "as I recall your telling of the story, you thought this somewhat strange."

"He looked a lot more like a rock or pop... I guess it was just his youth."

"Your subconscious mind is brilliant, yes."

"You're thinking," I said, "of course I would have to conjure up a gospel singer in order to bring about all that's happened."

"Can you deny this singing person," he said, "is the reason you're sitting here in Los Angeles today. You've known these friends for years, yes?"

"You think I dreamed all this up because I didn't have the balls to approach Skye and Dallas with… Look the play was their fuckin' idea!"

"Was it," he asked peering over his glasses? "Yet, someone had to physically put in the yellow highlights. Some mind had to envision this play, yes?"

"Can we talk about the woman?"

"There's not much here," he said; looking over my notes. "This last word, this could be significant."

"How so," I asked.

"You didn't finish it," said Dr. Epstein, "the writing trails into manic scribbling, looks like… personality."

I was out of my seat, suddenly perspiring, very anxious and moving. I don't remember leaving the office or the building. When I stopped hyperventilating I was lying in the middle of the sidewalk on Wilshire Boulevard.

"Now that is some strange shit," said Dallas after I told him the story, "you sure you're alright, Carson? Maybe we should get you checked out."

"I'm fine now, brother," I said, "thanks. Epstein's fitting me in tomorrow. I'm really sorry about all this, Dallas. I know this must be costing you a fortune."

"I'm worried, man," he said, "You just passed out. Maybe it was a seizure or something."

"No, I'm fine, Dallas, really. You think we could just keep this between ourselves. Skye's got enough to deal with."

"No way man, secrets are like poison. Skye's your friend, Carson. I hate lying and keeping things from him."

"He knows what's been happening?" I asked, "About why I came here, I mean?"

"You asked me not to say anything and I didn't," he said. "I'm not lying anymore, Carson. Besides he has to know something's going on with you. Epstein was his psychiatrist."

"I figured as much. Was, as in he no longer sees him?"

"No, he checks in with another guy when he's in Manhattan now," he said. "So, one minute you were talking with him and then, what?"

"I don't really remember much more than I already said man. Henry was parked across the street. Says he saw a few people gathering around, looked to see what was going on, and there I was laid out on the side walk."

"Maybe it was some kind of panic attack."

"Look, Dallas," I said, "I know you're concerned, but please can we get off this. I'll see Epstein in the morning, he's a doctor. So Skye's asking for a rewrite?"

"Yeah, scene two," he said, "says the dialogue is a little sketchy. Oh, and he thinks Anna is coming across as a primadonna playing dress-down."

"I think she's perfect," I said, "remember Linda from the park?"

"Do I remember her? Dude, that is her! No wonder Skye's not feeling the actress, he never liked Linda. I wonder if he's made that connection. What ever happened to her anyway?"

"Heroin."

"Oh, that's fucked up," he said, "damn."

"Maybe she cleaned up, I don't know. Remember her little boyfriend Andy?"

"Sort of, yeah, I remember that dude, hella skinny with freckles and red hair."

"Tech genius; drives a Lamborghini," I said. "I ran into him at a few gay clubs."

"Okay, so we need to talk about the singles," said Dallas, "so far it's going to be "We've Done Something Bad" for sure. That song is kick ass, man."

"Gospel," I asked.

"Well, not standing alone, that's for sure. We're working on how to package this thing, man. Stratton is a Gospel label; I don't want us veering off into other genres, this is Joey and his partner's vision. I'm just keeper of the flame."

"Joey White left everything to you for a reason," I said, "I'm so proud of you dude. The man knew what he was doing."

"I miss him, Carson. Joey was like a father to me," he said, "better than a father."

"This project, this play, be honest with me, Dallas, this is not just charity?"

"Carson, this is what people do, man," he said. "We love you, brother. You're a talented man who just happens to be our best friend. Of course we're going to help you. And by the way; Joey would absolutely love this. This is so the way he worked. C'mon man, you think he brought me out here and did all this because I was the best singer he'd ever heard?"

"I wish I could have met him," I said, "Damn, everything happened so quick. You guy's leaving the city I mean. What was it; a couple months after you met him?"

"There were circumstances propelling us, trust," he said. "Fuck; that was a strange set of circumstances, dude you got no idea!"

"What were you saying about secrets a couple minutes ago?"

"No secret," he said, "it's just that long before Skye's mother eventually paid to have me killed. She had flown her private dick out to San Francisco to plant heroin, cocaine and a .38 in my boots."

Chapter Seven

Dreaming about you

Dispatcher: "911, What is your emergency?"

Caller: "There's someone following me. Listen, I'm a psychiatrist; I left my office in Beverly Hills maybe ninety minutes ago. There's been someone following me since then, a woman."

Dispatcher: "Are you mobile, doctor?"

Caller: "Yes, yes, I'm in my car now. I first noticed this person as I left the parking garage of my office near Beverwill Drive, then again outside of the restaurant where I had dinner with my wife in Century City."

Dispatcher: "You're with your wife now?"

Caller: "No, I sent her back into the restaurant. We live there in Century City; I thought it best not to lead this person to our home. I'm driving east down Santa Monica Boulevard, I'm approaching Doheny Drive, I…

Note from Dispatcher: The sound of smashing glass, a brief scuffle, and then the doctor's screams…

"Why are you reading me this?" I asked detective Spencer as we sat in his office at the Beverly Hills police station, "I assume this is hard evidence, is this how the police work now?"

"Well, let's just say you're a very special witness," he said. "There's not a lot in the call, a few good points though. One, the person following him was a woman. Two, he became aware of her after just having left his office, and three, the time line."

"I was his last patient," I said.

"Bingo! According to the doctor's log you left his office just moments before he and his secretary a Mrs. Shelby closed his office for the day."

"You want to know if I saw anything, that it? Well, I do remember the session going over twenty minutes or so, and I remember Mrs. Shelby locking the door behind me. I didn't see anyone else as I left."

"Your session with the doctor when over a full twenty minutes," asked a second detective, "how often does that happen?"

"First time with me." I said, "I guess since I was the last... No, I know why, I didn't think of it at the time. Epstein must have been letting me run over deliberately. I had left a previous session abruptly."

"Why?" asked the second detective, his name was Johnson.

"Do I have to answer that," I asked turning to face Spencer? "I came here to help if I can, but I don't think you should be asking me about..."

"This was an expensive doctor's office," said Johnson, "why would you leave before your time was up?"

"What?"

"Okay, so we know about the incident last Wednesday," said Spencer, "you ran out of a session with the doctor, just after that you lost consciousness. Want to tell us what happened there?"

"What the hell does that have to do with anything?" I said, "Now I see why people want their fuckin' lawyers present! You think I had something to do with this?"

"We have to check things out," said Johnson, "we're the cops, right?"

"Okay so you didn't notice anything suspicious," said Spencer. "Were you parked in the garage?"

"What is this," I asked, "obviously if I were parked in the building garage, there'd be a witness or some record of it. No, I don't drive."

"A taxi then," asked Johnson.

"A driver drops me off and then..." I trailed off; I suddenly had an awful headache.

"Hey, you okay," asked Spencer, "Mr. Elliot, are you...?"

"I just need a minute," I said; clutching my forehead, "maybe a couple aspirin."

"Get him some aspirin and water," instructed Spencer.

After a few very long minutes; I said, "So I guess we just stumbled into why I was seeing Dr. Epstein."

"Headaches," asked Spencer.

"Migraines," I said, "debilitating migraine headaches. My doctors ran out of tests. They told me there's nothing; at least nothing physically wrong with me."

"Sick in the head, huh," said Johnson coming back into the room with a cup of water. I noticed several other cops standing just outside the door. "Forget about the fuckin' aspirin. I'd say a headache is the very least of your problems mister, or maybe you prefer Miss."

"What?"

"Enough of this bullshit," he said flinging the water into my face, "time to talk Miss Thing or whatever you call yourself when you're out killing people!"

"He's right Elliot," said Spencer, "I don't know what made you think you could do this in the middle of Santa Monica Boulevard and not be seen. We've got eleven witnesses so far that will swear they saw you bump Dr. Epstein's car with the stolen limo, smash his window, then shove that rusty tire iron through his eye socket!"

"That's a lie," I yelled.

"Eyeball and brain matter on one end of the weapon," yelled Johnson, "only one set of prints on the other, want to take a guess whose?! Even got the womanly Chanel shades you left at the scene. What a dumb shit!"

"No! I'm telling you, that's not what..." I said!

"Stand up Elliot," said Spencer presenting handcuffs as if by magic, "you're under arrest for the first degree murder of Dr. Randel Epstein."

"Nooooo....!"

"Carson, Carson!" it was Etna, "just dreamin', baby, everthang okay. Ma goodness, gotta say yo' body sho' nuf fava dis' here couch."

"Huh, what... I've been here the whole time," I asked coming awake, "I mean I haven't left the house, Etna?"

"Course not," she said, "where ya gon' go, can't even drive no car, Carson Elliot. Only way somebody comin' off dis hill is drivin' or ridin.' Musta been a terrible dream. Ya woke me right up out ma nap!"

"Yeah, yeah, I'm real sorry about that, Miss Etna. Was I screaming? Sometimes they seem so real."

"Etna understand, baby," she said. "Just give it a few mo seconds, everthang come back in focus. I use ta have mighty horrible dreams ma self, went on fo near a year after dat crazy doctor come near killin' me and both da' boys."

"It must have been horrible."

"Horrible sho'nuf, man ain't even know me gon' take ma life. They say that crazy fool killed ma Joey, hiptize him, make ma baby run on his runnin' machine til his heart plum give out on him. Den course somebody kill da' fool fo da' vestigation! Anyway, sleepin' come real hard fo' long time afta dat."

"I've been having some problems, Etna."

"Course ya are," she said, "ya thank ol' Etna blind. I no somethin' goin' on with ya, baby. Ya round yo' folk now, Carson, da' boys real crazy bout ya. Etna, love ya too, son. I's in da' business a takin' care a folk a long time. Dem head doctors don't know everthang, baby. Ya open up now, let folk know ya and care bout ya in."

"I've been seeing the shrink since I got here. It's these damn dreams; the click-off switch is just not working. I can't tell what's real half the time, I... If you weren't here just now, Miss Etna, I'd be walking around thinking I'd killed my doctor!"

"Ya mean ya remember ever thang real clear, like it really happened?"

"I thought it was because I was taking too much medication," I said; relieved that I was finally sharing this with someone outside of a doctor's office. Who would have thought that I'd be doing this with, Miss Etna Jackson? Of course Dallas knew the basics.

"Whatcha thank about, God, baby?"

"Huh?"

"Etna, ain't stutter," she said, "whatcha thank bout, Him?"

"I'm not sure I understand the question," I said, "but sure, I believe there is a, God, if that's what you mean."

"Ya thank our, God, got any power, I's mean right now in dis here present time?"

"Sure, I mean I guess so. I'm not a very religious person, Miss Etna."

"Me nether," she said, "folk in duh church get on ma last nerve, always messin' in otha folk business. Call dat Godly. Well, ol' Etna, done seen plenty nuff ta know bout, folk."

"Now, come on, Miss Etna, you know you never miss a Sunday, gotta be the only day I've ever heard you refuse to work."

"Well, I love, The Lord; sho nuff, gotta have ma day wit', Him! Love the sangin' and clappin', shoutin', and carryin' on in the church house too. And I gotta say, I love me some, Pasta Brown. Him, and, Pasta Cindy, too! Dey do a fine job preachin' da' word. But non a dat why I go ta church, baby, lease ways ain't da' main reason."

"It sounds like you have a good time," I said. "My family went regular when I was a kid. I always looked forward to Sundays back then."

"Well havin' a good time in the house is okay," she said, "Sho beat all dim otha places folk be goin'… Anyway, go a lot deeper den dat, baby. Carson Elliot, I wont ya ta know, God, been good ta me, we go a long, long way back. Well, bein' in the flesh like I am, lease fo da' moment, ma mind wonders here and dare, gotta be careful I don't never forget."

"Something happened? You've been sick?"

"Naw, so far ol' Etna healthy as a bull. Been plenty sick in ma head doh. Etna, marry da' worse kinda man, baby. Whoopin' on me, messin' wit' oda folk wives, drankin', stealin' ma little money, everthang, plus he real ugly. Don't rightly know what wrong wit' me don't see dat kinda bone ugly."

"You didn't have to marry, him," I asked? "I mean circumstances… you weren't…?"

"Yep, you right," she said, "sixteen year old and pregnant. Still don't splain why I eva open ma legs fo somebody dat ugly, den go marry him. I hada been real scurd, ma daddy not so good neda. Thank God, all ma chilin most fava me."

"How many children you have, Miss Etna?"

"Etna got fo babies, well, course day long way from babies now. Six grand chilin now, notha in da' oven. Dat be from ma daugta Rosemary, Lawd, have mercy, God, have truth, dat girl... woo... thank you, Jesus! Dat girl young, darn near gimme a heart attack three, fo' times. We had it real bad back dur near Mobile, baby. Darn fool man leave me wit' all dim babies; run off wit' da' mailman's wife. Well, I guess dat be the best part, him runnin' off I mean, weren't good fo nothin' no way."

"You raised your children alone," I said. "That must have been tough."

"Sho'nuff. Tough ain't even da' word fo it, baby. Bad nuff tryin' raise up three boy's wit' no man round, but dat Rosemary, well, dat girl da' one drove me to da' Lord so reckon dat da' way

thangs spoze ta happen."

"You guys lived out in the country, just outside of Mobile

right?"

"Devil come fo her she fifteen year old," she said.

"Rosemary a problem child, one dim kind real hard ta work wit' ya

know. Neva no why she so hard and mean, mouth all ways stuck

out like she mad bout somthin' all da' time. Me and ma Rosemary

hardly get along at all during dat time. Well, dat ol' devil see right

through the hardness. Rosemary like one dem fancy chocolates

come in a box; hard on da' outside, soft and chewy on da' inside.

Dat ol' Devil see her weakness."

"This Devil," I asked, "this was a guy?"

"No guy, pur evil what he was. Dat thang ruint a lot a young

girls, trick dey mind ta get'um way from dey folks. Some dem folk

neva hear from dey girls again."

"He'd hurt them?"

"Worse, put'um on da' street corner, make'um sell dey stuff," she said, dabbing her eyes with the sleeve of her blouse. "Etna, neva even know Rosemary talk to dat man, not fo it too late anyway."

"A pimp...Etna..."

"Dat be tha right name fo it all right," she said, "Etna, didn't know what ta do, baby. Couse I got ta tell ma boys, dey da' only mans in da' house. Etna, pray God dey don't kill'um, dem boys a mine have a hard time wit' da self control, specially ma big one Leroy. Ma friend, Miss Ernestine, tell me she see ma baby ridin' wit him. Darn fool ridin' round in a big ol' orange Cadillac, can ya magine ridin' round in somethin' like dat way out in da' country? White folk don't care. Dey know what he up to, long as he keep his eyes off da' white girls; dey don't care. I know dey thank it a Black problem. Wouldn't surprise me none dat ol' cracka sherf had somethin' do wit it, lettin' him run da' streets like dat. Anyway, I falls down on ma face; I's right beggin' the, Lord, pullin' ma hair out ma scalp, throwin' dirt an rocks all in ma face and mouth, I's real, real humble, baby. I tell, God, if He bring ma baby back home to me safe I praise him all ma left days…"

"Hey, wha'sup?" It was Dallas coming in through the kitchen.

"Hey, baby," said Etna, "me and Carson just havin' us a real good talk. He tellin' me how he can't wait ta come ta church wit' us in da' mornin', ain't dat right Carson?"

"Huh…well… yeah, of course," I said. "It's past time I see the great man work his magic."

"Pastor Brown, is a good dude, Carson," said Dallas, "you'll like him. Seems like every time you've been in town he's been out on the road somewhere. You'll get a chance to meet everybody, brother. Most of the Stratton folks you haven't run into yet and close to everybody else we know. We all go to the same place, man."

"Well, best get workin' on dinner," said Etna making her way to the kitchen, "gon' need one y'all get da' grill goin', barbeque tonight."

"So, how was work," I asked.

"Its work," he said, "got some pretty lame reviews on the project we dropped last month."

"Holy Bird," I asked. "Wow, I thought that whole CD was hot. Who blasted it?"

"Just a few folks on Amazon. Still, it's not a good sign. And it really got to, Scratch. He poured blood into that thing, man. One woman in Kansas thought the title cut was going to be about fried chicken. Actually demanded her money back," he laughed.

"The Holy Spirit came like a dove," I said, "damn, even I know that and I'm a heathen."

"Always a few nuts on that site. Now-a-days anybody can be a critic; it's just that there were quite a few. Even the good ones were at best lukewarm. Poor guy, he handpicked that group, produced the project with his own money. I hate to say it, but I just don't see that ship sailing. He's going to take a hit on this one."

"I take it that doesn't happen very often."

"Naw, not with, Scratch Wilson," said Dallas, "you know he produced "The City" right? Skye won't work with anybody else."

"Will I be meeting him tomorrow too?"

"Duh, Scratch is the music director; and nobody can touch him on that organ."

"Dallas, go on start da' fire," yelled Etna from the kitchen!

"Hello, Mrs. Shelby, Carson Elliot here. I know you won't be getting this message until Monday morning, so sorry for the late notice. I won't be able to keep my 3:00 appointment; nor will I be making any other appointments going forward. Please send my

final bill by mail. Thank you."

Chapter Eight

Church

"One Love Body of Believers Church," was huge, beautiful

on a par with contemporary Catholic Church architecture. A

modern steel and stained glass masterpiece located in the heart

of downtown Los Angeles. Of course on my first day we would

have to be late. Traffic had come to a complete stop several times

on the notorious LA freeways. As we entered the sanctuary the

Spirit must have smacked Dallas right in the face, he took off on

one leg down one of the many aisles. It seemed like the whole

church had drank from the happy juice jug just before we walked

in. The musicians hammered a rhythmic beat I'd heard all my life,

but never with such beauty in tone. There was a woman standing behind a microphone in the pulpit. It seemed like every time she'd open her mouth to say something The Holy Ghost (or whatever) would knock her lips shut and she'd be dancing.

"Don't be scurd, baby," said Etna holding my arm, "dis how we do it here."

"I know a little something about worship, Miss Etna," I said, "I ain't scurd." As she held on; Miss Etna and I started moving our feet too! Now that ol' girl could move them feet, shout and yell glory too. This part of the service went on for another fifteen minutes or so after we'd arrived. Finally the woman at the microphone was able to get the congregation back in to some semblance of order.

"Now yawl done danced right through the announcements," she said securing her wig as she spoke. "Make sure you read your bulletins, everything's in there. Praise team, c'mon!"

'You mean all that was before the cheerleaders?' I thought.

The raised choir stands to the left and right of the pulpit held at least a hundred singers. Now, eight more took center stage. We were able to get through the first and second songs beautifully. As luck would have it these were two of my all-time favorites. I actually knew the words. By the second verse of the third it was like the New Year's ball had just dropped in Times Square. The whole church it seemed had lost its collective mind once again.

"Well, Etna plain forget ta tell ya bout what happened," said Etna into my ear. "Youth choir bus was in a bad accident few days ago! Darn thang smashed inta a rail and flipped over."

"What?!"

"Not one dem chilin' hurt bad," she said, "ain't he a good G... hey, hey, hey..." She was dancing!

"That was a wonderful sermon, pastor," said Dallas taking the man's hand and hugging him tight, "as always of course."

"Good to see you, Dallas," said Pastor Johnny Brown, "And you must be Carson," he said extending his hand.

"A pleasure pastor," I said taking the man's hand. Suddenly, he was squeezing my fingers, his eyes locked into mine. It felt as though he was staring right into me!

"I see you," he said.

"Huh, what," I said pulling my hand away! "What the hell..."

"Pastor," said Dallas, "pastor is there something wrong?"

The man seemed in a trance, after several long awkward moments he returned to himself. "I'm sorry," he said, "too much work. Please, you guys have a seat. I need to throw a little water on my face.

As the man made his exit, Dallas turned towards me shrugging his shoulders high. We were sitting in Pastor Brown's stylish neo-classically designed office at the front of the church.

Dallas put his right index finger to his lips. After a few minutes the pastor stepped out of his adjoining restroom.

"Okay, so I hope you two will forgive an old man a senior moment," he said. "So, you're, Carson Elliot, I've been reading your books, excellent writing young man. I started with the one being adapted for the musical of course. Now I'm well into number three."

"Wow," I said, "thanks, pastor. That means a lot coming from you. You're some preacher. I was getting goosebumps in there."

"Of course a couple of your characters seem strangely familiar," said the pastor with a bit of humor in his voice. "Is that what those two were really like?"

"No," said Dallas.

"Yes," I said, "it's fiction of course, but everybody picks those two out pretty quick. Hey, at least they weren't the ones killing people, right?"

"So far," said Pastor Brown, "now don't be telling who the guilty or innocent are; I've got the whole series downloaded. So how's the play coming along?"

"Pastor sits on the board at Stratton, Carson," said Dallas, "he's been there since the very beginning."

"Who would have thought," said Pastor Brown. "Well, my brother in-law sure knew what he was doing. Young Dallas here has been doing a fine job, we're all so proud of him. Yep, he's the right man alright."

"It's been great working with my buddies," I said, "and of course I can hardly wait to see the novel performed. But, well I gotta tell you, pastor, that's a lot of work for what will likely be just a couple hours on stage."

"Let's not forget that sound track," said Dallas, "there's going to be at least two, maybe three top ten cuts on this CD."

"I hear this is something new for you, Carson," said Pastor Brown. "Sounds like you're off to a wonderful of a start, brother. I've heard some of the tracks; those are powerful lyrics, man."

"Well, I've been writing something since forever," I said, "but yeah, this is the first time working with music. It's kinda weird; I mean that so much can be done with just a few words."

"Wait till those royalty checks start coming in," said Dallas, "trust me this is just the beginning, brother."

"Dallas, I'm wondering if Carson and I might have a few minutes," asked Pastor Brown.

"Well, what was that about," asked Dallas as soon as the passenger door shut on his cranberry red '56 Corvette Stingray? Etna maneuvered hers just behind us.

"What's with all the Vettes," I asked as if I didn't already know the answer. Joey White had left his cherished collection of

Corvettes to, Dallas, Etna, and his brother, Pastor Brown. Of

course, virtually everything else came to Dallas. Pastor Brown was

already a very wealthy man.

"Screw the cars dude," said Dallas, "what just happened

back there?"

"You mean that weird thing with the handshake," I asked.

"That too," he said. "C'mon Carson, what did the man want

to talk about?"

"The books."

"Bullshit," I said, "c'mon dude!"

"Okay, so he wanted to pray with me."

"Huh, you guys were in there for close to an hour."

"He wanted to pray and he prayed very hard," I said,

"worked himself into quite a frenzy. Look, I'm pretty sure it's

something like what goes on between a shrink and his patient.

You want to know more you're going to need a warrant detective."

"It's not that, it's just that..."

"Let it go Dallas, I know you're just looking out for me, brother. Thanks for bringing me today, this was great. I want to talk about something else, there was a guy; walked in on us at the very end of our little session."

"Oh, that was, Scratch," he said, "I tried to stop him. I guess you didn't recognize him; Scratch, was the man on the organ this morning. He's part of the family."

"The record producer, guy?"

"Yep; he's also music director for the church, why?"

"I don't know," I said, "seemed kinda nice."

"He's straight."

"What, I didn't say anything about..."

"Right, well I'm pretty sure the man is straight. Divorced now but he's got two kids. Can't say I blame you for noticing though, that face and can you believe that damn body, trust me; everybody notices, Mr. Scratch Wilson."

"He invited me to coffee tomorrow after I meet with the pastor."

"Huh?"

"Oh, Pastor Brown, wants to meet with me tomorrow."

Oh, these mothers are really trying it! First that goody two shoes muse freak shows up, then the quack-a-roo head doctor starts poking around. Now he's got a damn preacher praying over me! I don't know why but I think this one could be the most dangerous. I thought he actually saw me today, that's what he said "I see you." No one's ever seen me, and trust me they never want to. This preacher freak had better stay in his own lane, be a shame if that big fancy church of his went up in a blaze of glory.

Oops, did I just say that?

He called and cancelled on the shrink, says he's not coming

to see him anymore. What's he up to? Mr. Carson Elliot has been

making me very uncomfortable here lately, he'd better back off, I

mean it! The last thing any of them want to see is me pissed off!

I'm getting there, I'm getting real close.

"So, I hear you've known the guys a long time," said Scratch

Wilson. He was a beautiful, muscular, bi-racial man of somewhere

between thirty and thirty five, my age and definitely my type. We

were sitting in a little café just around the corner from "One

Love," I wasn't sure why he wanted to talk to me, and I wasn't

sure why he was making me blush like some silly school girl every

time he opened his mouth. Dallas had said the man was straight,

but... well I'll just leave it there at "but." Pastor Brown had to

reschedule as one of his deacons had had a mild heart attack the previous night. Scratch suggested I come on downtown anyway, our coffee date became lunch.

"Yeah, since our early twenties," I said, "we were all 'Haight street' boys for a while. That was before Joey White came to town of course."

"You ever meet Joey?"

"Naw, came close a couple times. I wish I could have met the man. Heard a lot about him of course, that's real fucked up what happened."

"He was a good dude," he said, "Joey and Dwayne gave me my break, actually they gave me my career."

"I hear you're one of the best producers in gospel music," I said. "You're the man, the way I hear it."

"Those guys made it happen; trust me. Now it looks like it may be your turn, brother."

"Actually, I'm a novelist; I don't know anything about music."

"Yet, I hear that musical of yours is going to make quite a splash. I'm sure you realize you guys are breaking new ground for Stratton, this is going to be a first."

"It was Skye's idea," I said.

"Really? That's not the way I heard it. Are you being modest, Carson? You don't have to be, you're one of us now."

"No really, the musical was totally Skye's idea. Okay, so here's how it happened. I mean if you want to... am I being a bore?"

"No, keep talking," he said, "I like your voice and I like watching your lips move."

"Slut," yelled the muse waking me from a sound sleep (I think.) "You're cheating on me!"

"What, what the hell," I said, "what are you..."

"Oh, wake up Carson, I'm only kidding," he said. "So you've met a man, I'm in shock."

"I've met plenty of m..."

"Really, when? Go on tell me the last time you went on a date?"

"First off, how can you be waking me up when you only live in my dreams? Second, it wasn't a date. The guy's a record producer, he works with the company. I met him in the pastor's office thank you very much."

"And all of that is relevant; because," he said? "Well, just in case you really are that blind and naïve, the man has 'the hots' for you."

"I'm not so..."

"What kind of grown man tells another grown man he likes watching his lips move? C'mon dude."

"What do you want, Muse," I asked. "I should be sleeping. Skye's back in the morning, we have to start putting this thing together."

"Okay, so the play's coming along nicely, what about the book?"

"You've got to be kidding; you do realize the sets are being built as we speak. They're probably already printing the fucking tickets."

"All very nice," he said, "I need you writing. What you don't seem to understand, my friend, is that we won't always be together. Write Carson; get down as much as you can. The very foundation of your future is being laid, right now. There will be no 401K, my friend, this is it. Keep writing, Carson, don't stop."

"This new book," I said, "it's not going to be part of the series is it?"

"How would I know, you're the writer."

"Yeah, right, so is it? C'mon, man, or whatever you are; every time I try to link it in any way to the 'perfect place' I end up stuck, and then it's all about the delete key."

"I thought my initial inspiration took you in a different direction," he said, "at least that's what you told me back in San Francisco."

"Yeah, but where. You're falling down on your job, Muse."

"Am I? Why did you cancel with, Epstein?"

"So is it that you know everything, or some things; what?"

"I think you should go back," he said. "Actually, I think it's real important that you go back, Carson."

"Something happened," I said, "so it looks like you don't have access to everything that goes on inside my head."

"What are you talking about, what happened?"

"Maybe it was just a stupid nightmare, shook me up pretty bad though. Hell, I still remember the details now, scary."

"What happened, man, I'm serious."

"I dreamed I killed Epstein," I said, "shoved a rusty tire iron through his eye, his brain, then out the back of his head."

"What else?"

"Well, I... I caught my image in his side view mirror. It was weird, dude, I... I looked like a woman."

"That fucking bitch," yelled the muse. "She's trying to scare you off, man. Epstein must have been getting too... Same reason she wants me dead."

"What are you talking about, Muse, you're freaking me out!"

"Bianca."

Chapter Nine

The Demon Slayer

"Hey, come on in," said Pastor Brown; greeting me as I stepped into his office, "I'm real sorry for having to cancel on you yesterday, an emergency."

"That's okay," I said. "How's the deacon?"

"Not great, this was his second heart attack in the last couple years. Deacon Baker, a good man and a good friend, please add him when you pray tonight. So, I guess you're wondering why I asked you to come down here, Carson."

"Kinda."

"Kinda, as in you've got some idea?"

"We both know something strange happened on Sunday, pastor," I said. "I couldn't help but notice that when we prayed alone together you kept your arms folded tight around you, if I didn't know better I'd think you were afraid to touch me."

"Afraid, is not the right word," he said. "Are you a believer, Carson?"

"Yeah, sure, I believe in, God."

"The Trinity?"

"I'm not exactly sure I believe everything the way the church would have me believe it, Pastor Brown," I said. "I'm not even sure I should claim a perfect grasp of understanding based on bible stories. I don't mean that disrespectfully, pastor, I understand it's the job of the preacher to preach the book."

"An intelligent man," he said. "I don't think a man's intelligence is of much use in the kind of fight you're in brother."

"Fight?"

"Oh yes, it's a fight, let's be clear there. I'd like very much to help you whip this thing you're up against, brother. But in the end I don't have much power; nothing like the kind you're going to need."

"I'm not following you, pastor," I said, "sure I've got a few issues, I think most people have a few things they need to work on but..."

"Let's not waste time, Carson, we've got work to do. First up; this "I believe in, God" stuff is not going to work, at least not in your case, there's not nearly enough power in so general a statement. Tell me about Jesus."

"Now, here we go."

"Here we go where? This is a Christian church; I'm a Christian and a Christian pastor. Can I assume you're Christian as well?"

"Yeah, but... well, you know, I..."

"Right," he said, "well, the first thing we need to do is figure out exactly what a Christian is, more to the point what it means to wear, His, cross."

"Could we just talk like regular people for just a bit, Pastor Brown," I said, "I mean before we get into all the religious stuff. You're right; I believe I'm in serious trouble, I..."

"Yes, we'll talk, and I'll counsel you, brother, and of course we're going to pray together. In fact I have a feeling we're going to be doing a lot of praying. All of those will happen AFTER you've read the book of John and at least one of the other gospels."

"Huh, but you don't even know..."

"I know you have a demon, I've seen it," he said. "This is not a game, Carson, this thing is dangerous, in a millisecond I saw violence. Read the books, brother, they serve a purpose."

"Pastor Brown, with all due respect, I'm thirty-four years old, was involved in church for a lot of those years. You think I'm not already familiar with the, New Testament?"

"Are you? Do what I've asked of you, brother, don't call me until you're ready?"

"Huh, okay… Alright, so the books are pretty short, can't we do it now?"

"No, not us, you," he said standing. "Even the power of, Jesus Christ, can't help you brother if you don't believe in your heart that, He, can. I'm hoping I'll hear from you tomorrow.

"Okay, quiet everybody," yelled Skye from third role center seat! "Keep in mind; this will be the last rehearsal before opening. If you screw anything up, keep moving! That would include sprains and/or fractures people! Alright chorus, thirty seconds, on the green light!"

He was yelling over the already playing introduction. In a moment heavy drapes parted center stage. Skye could only sit through the opening dance number before rushing backstage; he and Dallas sang their first of three duets during the first act.

The Overton Theater was huge and quite beautiful, four-hundred-eighty seats, three-quarters of which were pre-sold for opening night. We were expecting a full house by curtain. Oh, how I wish I could have been up there with them. While it's true I recognize and fully accept I'm not the least gifted with any sort of performance talent, that doesn't mean a man can't fantasize. Twenty-two dancers fill the stage for the opening number. It was spectacular, everything was spectacular; the dancers, singer/actors, choreography, the sets, everything came together in such a polished and magical way. I never dreamed I would ever be involved in something so... When Skye and Dallas took to the stage I teared up.

Just as the final curtain came down he leaned up from the seat behind me.

"Congratulations," he said holding my shoulders while kissing the top of my head. "Looks like you've written Stratton's very first hit musical, my friend!"

So much for the, "he's straight," argument. "Scratch, where did you come from," I asked. "Hey, how long have you been…"

"I've been here a while," he said, "didn't want to distract you. Now pull yourself together, Carson, we've got a surprise for you."

"We?" Scratch Wilson then took me by the hand, this was surprise enough. As we stepped into the green and black art deco lobby of the theater, Dallas, Skye, and many of the cast members where crowded around a huge red draped something or other.

"What's all this," I asked of no one in particular?

"Okay," yelled Skye, "one, two, three!" The draping was pulled off, everyone broke into a jazzed up version of "For He's a Jolly Good Fellow!"

It was so beautiful, my books, my children, all five of my novels! There were hundreds of copies; all stacked on varying levels against a miniature replica of the musical's set. I did know there would be book signings at the intermission and end of each performance; I never dreamed it would be so elaborate a setting.

"Let's give it up for the architect," yelled Dallas, "Mr. Scratch Wilson, yeah…"

"You? You, did this for me," I said turning to face him? "I don't know what to…"

He put his arms around me, pulled away just a bit, and then he kissed me. I mean, he kissed me!

The room erupted with applause.

"Thank you, for seeing me again, doctor," I said.

"It's good to see you again, yes, yes," said Dr. Epstein. "So, let's not waste time, you will tell me why you chose to stop coming, yes?"

"So much has happened, doctor; I don't know where to start."

"You evade the question, yes, yes. Okay, so begin where you will, Carson."

"The muse is still around, not as much as before, but he's still popping in. I've kinda gotten use to him."

"You say this casually," said Epstein, "you have a better understanding?"

"I guess. He's a dream and a daydream, tells me he's not always going to be around. Figured I'd just take him at his word. It's not like he's trying to hurt me, in fact..."

"Go on."

"This thing is a lot more complicated than... I've got serious, maybe even dangerous problems, Dr. Epstein. I need help."

"The medications, what are you taking now?"

"Nothing," I said, "as in, absolutely nothing."

"Go on," he began writing in his notebook.

"That fire in San Francisco. Does either of us really believe that was just a coincidence, doctor? I mean what are the odds of me being there, on the scene, right there in the middle of it. Why would an empty apartment, an apartment that had been empty for a couple weeks, which just happened to be my apartment just spontaneously, burst into flames?"

"That case, the case for arson, it is still open, yes?"

"C'mon Epstein, you're not really going to pretend they weren't here?"

"There are ethical rules," he said, "boundaries that must be maintained. Since you have brought this up, yes, yes, I will tell you. Arson investigators have come here to the office."

"And?"

"I wouldn't see them, they know the laws as well as I. Doesn't stop them from trying. A warrant for something like what we're talking about, not likely."

"I wasn't lying when I said I knew nothing about the fire doctor, you've got to believe me, I..."

"Yes, yes, there is work to be done," he said. "I think it's time we consider hypnosis."

"Oh, no, that will never happen. Not a chance."

"The incident with your friends, I am familiar with..."

"The incident," I said! "Is that what you would call what happened with that sick motherfucker? Well, that's just never going to happen. We may as well move on."

"But you want me to help you, yes? Surely you don't think something like…"

"HE SAID BACK OFF, ASSHOLE!"

"Carson I'm only trying to help you understand…"

"DAMN, ARE YOU HARD OF FUCKIN' HEARING OR JUST OLD AND STUPID?!"

"Carson. Carson Elliot?"

"NO, NO, YES, YES, NO, FUCKIN' NO, YES, YES! THAT MUST HAVE BEEN SOME SET OF SCHOOLS YOU WENT TO. YES? FUCK!"

"Tell me your name," said Dr. Epstein.

"WELL, IT SURE AS HELL AIN'T WHUSSY ASS, CARSON ELLIOT!"

"You're female?"

"BOY, YOU REALLY ARE SMART! MY NAME IS BIANCA AND DON'T PRETEND YOU DON'T KNOW ABOUT ME!"

"Why now, Bianca?"

"WHY THE HELL NOT! LOOK DUMB, DUMB, I'M ONLY GOING TO SAY THIS ONCE. THIS IS OVER. IF WHUSSY MAN DRAGS ME BACK INTO THIS OFFICE AGAIN, I'LL BE BRINGING GAS CANS AND A FLAME WITH ME!"

"It was you," said Epstein, "you caused the fire, yes?"

"BINGO! KILL THE YES, YES, CRAP OLD MAN, GETS ON MY FUCKIN' NERVES! OF COURSE I BURNED THAT DUMP, YOU THINK WHUSSY MAN..."

"Why? Why would you burn his apartment? What did you destroy, Bianca?"

"AM I GOING TO HAVE TO HURT YOU, OLD MAN? MAYBE BURN SOME OF THOSE WHISKERS AND WRINKLES OFF YOUR FUCKIN' SKULL! I TOLD YOU, BACK THE FUCK OFF!"

"Carson, Carson Elliot," yelled Epstein! "Carson Elliot!"

"YOU BITCHES DESERVE EACH OTHER! YOU'VE BEEN WARNED, ASSHOLE, BACK OFF!"

I felt as though I was waking from a deep sleep. I knew something was wrong, something had happened. Epstein was staring at me like I had three heads. Why was I sweating?

"Carson?"

"What happened," I asked, "Oh, God, what's wrong with me, doctor?"

"You're okay, yes, yes," said Epstein; holding his stare, "you're okay, my friend."

"I don't remember... you spoke with the, muse, he was here?"

"No, Carson this is highly unusual, I need to ask you to remain here in this office while I... I need to consult with a colleague."

"Are you calling the police, Dr. Epstein?"

"No, no, of course not. You will wait, yes?"

"Swear to me you're not calling the police."

"A Perfect Place to Hide," opened with a bang. Not one bad review, not even one bad remark appeared in print as far as I could tell. Full house for all three L.A. performances, the Overton Theater was not eager to see us move on, and in fact had presented a very generous offer for the show to continue. We had to decline as we were under contract for the following six weeks. The next stop was, San Diego. To be honest, I didn't want to go. The novel and CD concession could easily be manned by someone else, but when my greedy little ass-wipe of a publishing house saw the receipts for just three nights...

Something significant had happened in Dr. Epstein's office. Although he was vague and had insisted we not open up a discussion with limited time and other patients waiting in his lobby. I knew something important had happened, that look on his face, the way he seemed to be studying me in the final

moments of the session. It wasn't until Mrs. Shelby started

penciling me in for the following day that it dawned on me, 'oh,

shit,' we were on the road in the morning.

"You never finished the story, Etna," I said while continuing

to pack my luggage as she folded.

"Which one dat, baby," she said, "Etna, just startin' ta get

old now."

"You were telling me about your daughter, Rosemary."

"Oh yeah, were I leave off da' story, baby."

"That guy, a man was trying to..."

"Okay, like I's sayin', I come to da', Lord, right beggin' dat

night," she said, "Rosemary, missin', clothes gone out da' closet. I

know she wit' dat geechee. I pray, God, please brang her back, let

her mind not be ruined. Course I tell ma boys go out lookin'."

"They found her?"

"Don't do nar bitta good ta rush da' story, baby. Well, everthang go bad ta worse. Ma boys split on dey search, weurt'cha know it be Leroy find'em. Ma boy, Leroy, eighteen year old, darn near three hundred pounds. Way he tell it, he only brang his daddy's old shot gun, case the geechee try to run. Tho' he young; Leroy way too big fo runnin'"

"Somebody got hurt?"

"Dat where, God, come in, baby. Leroy corner dat fool sneakin' out da' back winda at da' Motel 6. Ma Leroy say da' fool come at him wit' a switch blade knife. He wern't plannin' on killin' him, but he sho'nuf pulled da' trigga."

"Oh, my God, Etna..."

"Dat ol' shotgun his daddy left behind lock up on him, nothin' come out da' barrow."

"Wow, that's some stor..."

"Geechee, still got da knife," she continued, "he tryin' real hard ta put it in Leroy! Den, bam, he drop on da ground! Rosemary brang him down wit' a 2 by 4 to da' back his head. She kill him dead!"

"She killed him?"

"Sho'nuf, kill'um dead as a do' nail. Ya ask me dat girl done done da' world a big fava."

"Oh, my God, Etna, what happened!"

"I's get da' call from dat ol' cracka sheriff I told ya bout," she said. "He say get ma self down da' Motel 6 right quick. Baby, ya know, I get dar, see ever thang happened, I real close to ma heart give out on me. Leroy sittin' in da' back of da' police car, Rosemary ova on da' porch in front da' motel room. Dat geechee laid out... oh it real bad baby, I know he dead cause dey got da' blanket ova his face, blood soak all da' way through. I know ma family ova now, I cryin' close ta steria."

"Self-defense, she was just trying to..."

"God change his name dat night," she said.

"Huh," I said, "whose name, you said he was dead, right?"

"No, da' sheriff, fo' dat night Etna neva got nothin' good ta say bout da' man, always da' cracka or worse. I's never even know his name. Well, afta dat night, he always, Sheriff Reid, I's ask him ta call me, Etna."

"What happened?"

"He tell, ol' Etna, course I wernt too old back den, say, "Well mam, it looks like dis here city fella went and got himself robbed and killed by a couple drifters," he pause, look me right in ma face. "Take ya children home, Miss Etna."

"Wow."

"Everthang change afta dat' night, 'specially wit, Rosemary. Fact we all, ma whole family, come regulars down at da' church. Rosemary, end up marrying da' pasta's oldest boy, now he da' pasta. Dey got two boys and anotha in da' oven. Now, you go on

tell me dat ain't, God!"

Chapter Ten

Back in the city

This was it, opening night at the Orpheum Theater in San Francisco. I was coming home in style, four nights at the Orpheum, who would have thought. A year earlier a successful musical production was not even on the radar, in fact. Is that really the truth? I don't know, maybe Epstein had it right from the beginning. Not only was the muse musical, 'that voice,' but he also just happened to perform only gospel music, and of course I just happen to know Skye and Dallas who just happen to be in the gospel music business. Then of course he would have to have been homeless so I could move him into my building and my life;

which is where this whole novel/music business really got started. Then... there are just so many thens, now here we all are back in the city. I wondered if any of the old gang from the park would be in the audience...

Bang, bang, bang! "Hello," I said opening the door of my room at the eighth street Holiday Inn, "knocking kinda loud and kinda early aren't you?"

There were four suited men standing in the doorway, cops, no doubt about that.

"Carson Elliot," said the one closest to me while holding up a badge, "you are, Carson Elliot?"

"Yes, I'm Carson," I said, "is there a problem?"

"Yeah, you could say that," said a second policeman, "step out of the room sir."

"What?"

"Step out of the room, sir," he repeated while presenting a pair of handcuffs, "keep your hands in front of you."

I complied. "What's this about, officers? I..."

"Bet you can make a damn good guess," said the first officer. "Put your hands on top of your head clasping your fingers, no sudden moves."

'That damn apartment fire,' I thought. *'They must have been waiting for... they sure didn't look like arson investigators.'* "Hey, don't you need a warrant or something?"

"Never fly without one," said a third cop holding out an unfolded document. It was from Los Angeles.

"Are you here as my father or my attorney," I asked. We were sitting in a tiny interview room at 850 Bryant Street, the San Francisco County Jail.

"Attorney for the moment," said the Republican. "Carson, for the love of God... Who was this, Dr. Epstein? Were you seeing... "

"You probably know more than I do. I'm in big trouble, dad. What have they told you?"

"For openers; you're being charged with the confirmed arson at our building," he said, "that will at least buy us some time here in the city. You told me then you had nothing to do with it, I need you to tell me that again, son."

"I can't, dad. I can only say I have absolutely no memory of..."

"Most likely you'll be charged with first degree murder," he said. "That's why the L.A. cops were a part of your arrest. Take your time, Carson; let's start with how you knew this, Dr. Epstein?"

"I started seeing him soon after I arrived in LA. Dallas, set me up with him, I was having problems, dad."

"Delusions?"

"Yeah, well you know my story," I said, "just as sick as…"

"Go on, Carson; our time is limited."

"Well, I figured I was overmedicating, again. Epstein, was no pill pusher. He was actually a very good shrink. I started seeing him."

"This man's office was in Beverly Hills," he said. "How could you afford something like that?"

"So you do know a few things."

"I've seen the warrant and I've spoken with two of your friends," he said, "actually that was right here in the outer lobby. They were under the impression they could bail you out. That won't happen, not with the L.A. charges pending. You'll be arraigned on Monday morning. "

"Dallas and Skye are here?"

"Actually it's, Dallas, and another guy, I don't know him. I think he's with the record company."

"Scratch?"

"Yeah, that's him, that's some kinda name. So your friends knew this, Doctor, was that personally or professionally?"

"He was, Skye's, psychiatrist for a while," I said, "all that trouble a couple years back. They were picking up the tab. Damn, I can't believe this has actually happened, this is no fucking dream!"

"What's that supposed to mean?"

"It's really, really, complicated, dad. I can't give you solid answers because I really don't… How's, mom?"

"Stay focused," he said sternly, "what do you mean by 'it's no dream?'"

"I dreamed I'd killed him a couple months back," I said. "It shook me up really bad. So bad in fact that I called his office to cancel our next appointment, I'd decided not to see him again."

"But you did see him again?"

"Yes, I did. I'm a very sick person, dad, a lot sicker than we..."

"Okay, so this is what's going to happen, Carson," he said, "First, and listen to me well, you're not going to say anything about this case to anyone, not to cops and especially not to any inmate. This place is crawling with rats, believe me I know."

"They've got me in an isolated cell."

"An old cop trick," he said, "five to one you'll be getting a special cell mate tonight, don't say anything even remotely concerning your case to that person; keep conversation to a bare minimum. I don't care what he says or looks like, there's a good chance he'll be testifying in your trial. I'll retain a criminal attorney for you by tomorrow morning, after that it will be him communicating with you in this way. Think hard, son; is there something else you need to tell me now? Whatever you say; I can't be compelled to testify."

"You're asking me if I did this," I said. "I think maybe you're afraid to ask me straight out."

"There's got to be some kind of evidence, son, they wouldn't send cops up here with a warrant if..."

"I didn't do it," I yelled! "I could never kill anybody, dad, you must know that!"

"But you know something," he said. "Carson, I know you know more than you're..."

"Not now dad, I can't!"

There was a buzzing sound, accompanied by a blinking red light on the wall over the door.

"Not a word to anybody, Carson." said my father standing, "Remember what I've told you."

"You look like shit," said the muse. "I'm real sorry this has happened to you, Carson."

"Really," I said, "how about, Epstein? How are you feeling about what happened to him? It was you that said I should see him again, right?

"If it makes you feel better to blame me, go ahead. I'll take the heat."

"I had stopped seeing him! The man was in the clear, dammit!"

"It's not over," he said.

"What?"

"Think about it, she's got to be right here with us, right?"

"Alright, enough of the games, dude! I'm facing life, maybe even the fucking death penalty! You know something, say it, or leave me the fuck alone!"

"You've got a multiple personality disorder," he said.

"Technically I guess I'm one of them."

"Technically?"

"It's different with us. You know me, we're able to

communicate. I'm not a doctor, Carson; I thought, Epstein, could

help us, it's the only reason I said... I never dreamed it could come

to this."

"You mean help me don't you, after all you don't really

exist," I said. "Nobody's going to death row but me. So you're

telling me I've got some murderous sick bitch living in my brain,

that it?"

"Something's not right about all this, Carson."

"NOT RIGHT! What the... You can go now."

"Something's not right," he repeated. "I knew about the

fire! Do you understand what I'm saying, I couldn't stop or do

anything about it, but I knew."

"What are you saying?"

"Dr. Epstein, was drugged, zip-tied to a chair, and then shish kabobed with a blow torch. How could I not know that? I mean not know anything, sense anything, c'mon, dude."

"Hey, shut the fuck up, asshole," yelled a voice from another cell! "Ain't nobody tryin' ta hear that bullshit all motha fuckin' night!"

"Hey," said Dallas through a phone line from the other side of wire meshed glass, "I don't know what to say, man. How are you, Carson?"

"I think I may starve to death," I said, "I can't eat the shit they give us in here. Thanks for coming, Dallas."

"Everybody sends their love," he said, "they're only going to let you have two visits today though. Dallas, what do you need me to do? We'll do anything to help, brother."

"Well, the first thing you can do is finish the show! Second; try to keep this out of the papers."

"Too late for that."

"You mean…"

"Second page of the, Chronicle. It will be all over the LA papers by tomorrow morning, sorry."

"You know these pigs actually search your asshole before throwing you in here."

"We don't have a lot of time, Carson," he said, "Scratch, wanted to come really bad, he and Skye are out in the lobby."

"I thought I could see two people today."

"Yeah, that's not going to be either of those two though. You remember me telling you about the ex-cop who broke our case wide open."

"Yeah, Derrick Samuel. Works for 'One Love, Church' right? He's here?"

"He's the best, Carson; Pastor Brown, flew him up overnight."

"This is a real mess, Dallas," I said, "I'm so sorry for getting you guy's involved. That poor man, all he wanted to do was help me. You guys sent me to him; please tell Skye I had nothing to do with this, Dallas, I swear."

"Looks like it happened the night before we left L.A." he said, "I wonder what took them so long. I mean if they really think you had something to do with it shouldn't they have..."

"Those two L.A. cops, they looked kinda familiar."

"That's what Scratch said, he thinks maybe they've been following the show. In fact, he's pretty sure one of them had been fronting as a photographer for the promoter."

"So they've been talking to the cast and crew?"

"Yeah," said Dallas, "not only that, I talked to Miss Etna this morning, she was just leaving the Beverly Hills police station. She said they threatened to arrest her for obstruction of justice."

"Oh, my God, Dallas, you've got to believe me, I don't know anything about…"

"I believe you're telling the truth as best you can, brother," he said, "I also know a little about what you've been going through lately. Dammit, they must have something, Carson."

"I've got an attorney."

"Your dad?"

"My dad's a corporate attorney," I said. "Besides, no way would a judge allow him to represent me. The guy's name is, Benton, Clarence Benton; no doubt he'll be contacting you guys."

"Anything you want us to say or not say?"

"Just be honest, Dallas, the last thing I want is to suck you and Skye into this hole with me. What's going on with his dad?"

"They're offering him a deal if he pleads on two counts of first degree."

"He could get out?"

"Right, the deal is for forty-two years," he said, "which means if everything went smoothly he could get out just in time for his funeral, not likely though. I sure hope you've got the right guy, man."

"Seems competent, he was here a couple hours ago," I said. "This arson thing is the very least of it though. What they all want is to get me back to L.A."

"The show closes tonight of course," said Dallas on a lighter note. "Scratch says he's staying, damn; what did you do to that man? I'm still tryin' to wrap my head around him being interested in dudes; seems like he's a lot more than just interested in you, man."

"He's sweet," I said, "You know he's got to be wondering though, Dallas. Man hardly knows me."

"All I know is his nose is wide open; all he talks about is, Carson Elliot. That started before we left L.A."

"I think I may be falling in love with him, Dallas. This is great timing, huh?"

And so it went. I was arraigned on the arson charge based on circumstantial evidence. Before the judge would allow me to plead he'd ordered a psychological evaluation which actually became two. The first psychiatrist had to concede that he was out of his league. Apparently he'd caught a fleeting glimpse of the personality named, Bianca. Considering what had happened to the last psychiatrist to encounter her, and also considering something she apparently said to him in that moment he decided it best for him and for his young family to pass the case on to a more seasoned professional. The second doctor encountered no such person. His recommendation was that I be tried and treated like any other criminal. Of course, none of the players in this case with the exception of the insurance company had any real interest

in the outcome of a simple case of arson where not a single

person had been injured. I was offered a deal and quickly

convicted of a slightly lesser charge. Sentenced to three years'

probation on a misdemeanor I was released and then immediately

rearrested and handed over to L.A. Homicide detectives.

"Hello, Derrick," I said from behind a Plexiglas wall in the

visiting room of the L.A. county jail. "The food is even worse

here."

"Okay, so I've got what they have against you," he said. "I'm

afraid it's not looking good, Mr. Elliot."

"Please, don't call me that," I said; mentally preparing

myself for the worse. Derrick Samuel, was the full-time chief of

security at "One Love Body of Believers Church," he also worked

for Stratton Records when needed and was the primary reason,

Etna, Skye, and Dallas, had not met with untimely deaths two years prior. A middle-aged single Irishman with brown hair and a thick red mustache, Derrick, had been a sergeant with L.A.P.D. until the botched case resulting in the death of, Joey White's, partner, Dwayne Brown, landed him on a desk. Feeling the man had been treated unfairly and used as a public scapegoat, Pastor Brown, had offered him a position. When trouble came to visit two years back, Derrick, was given the job of protecting, Dallas, and all those around him. "So what have they got?" I asked.

"Tapes," he said, "and a witness."

"What? How do you know this?"

"I spent most of my adult life on the force; I've got a few friends."

"How can they have a witness when I didn't…"

"The tapes are more important at this point," he said. "The witness, a, Mrs. Shelby, can only offer hearsay, most likely inadmissible as evidence. You know who she is of course?"

"Yeah, sure, Dr. Epstein's, secretary and receptionist, she saw or heard something?"

"Worse, she taped your last session with the doctor."

"What! What the... Is that even legal?"

"I'm not a lawyer, Carson. She's also willing to swear she heard you threaten to kill him, 'burn the hair and wrinkles off his skull,' something like that."

"I never said anything like..."

"It's on the tape."

"Well, the fuckin' tape is wrong!"

"This Shelby woman, she can testify that she admitted you into his office, that moments later the doctor hit a buzzer signaling her to record the session and that you came out of the office alone."

"He was still alive, I hadn't touched him."

"True. Tell me about, Bianca."

Chapter Eleven

I love you

Hey, Scratch.

Thanks for the letters, brother. It's hard to believe I still have your attention. Everything is such a mess! Here I finally meet a guy like you, now all this. It's all so crazy, man. Of course I can't say much about the case. Inmates don't have a right to privacy. They read all my mail coming and going. I can only say that Derrick Samuel is on the case full time now. He tells me he knows you. Seems like a real competent dude, I just wish I could help him more. I only know what I know, Scratch, which isn't a whole lot. But I really do need to stop with all that for right now.

I was able to see, Pastor Brown, yesterday. He came in with my attorney. Can you believe we actually had to convince these people that I'm not a suicide risk? Whoopee, I can keep my sheets and jail clothes, still in a cell by myself though. I think about you a lot, Scratch, in fact you're all I seem to think about anymore. You are a beautiful ray of light shining into my black hell. I look forward to our visit. Pray for me, Scratch, pray for us. I lo... I'll save that for when we're together. Carson.

Elliot, get dressed," yelled a guard right after my morning slop had been pushed through a tray slot in the solid steel door of my humble abode, "attorney visit!"

"You're not playing it straight with me, Carson," said my new attorney, Ralph Walberg. "How can you expect me to defend you if..."

"Cut the bullshit, Walberg," I said, "what is it now?"

"These tapes from the shrink's office, you have to know what's on there. I'm telling you, Carson, if the prosecution can get those in..."

"You've heard them?"

"I've heard the last one made," he said, "apparently there are several more. What I've already heard is more than enough to convict on circumstantial. Our only hope is to suppress."

"Derrick, told me about the tape made the night before we left LA," I said, "I didn't realize there were more."

"Probably not admissible, this last one is where our focus needs to be. You threatened to kill him."

"That's what I hear."

"Not just that, Carson, you threatened to kill him in exactly the way he was killed."

"I know you don't believe a fucking thing I've told you." I said, "I don't remember, man, fuck! What, you think I'm trying to outsmart somebody?"

"Okay, okay, so it's going to have to be a psychological defense, I think we're all on the same page there. Just be advised, even if we can prove the existence of this other personality, this Bianca, it doesn't mean they let you go."

"I thought you said you'd only be hanging around for a little while," I said. "This is getting kinda old don't you think?"

"Actually, that's not what I think at all," said my muse. "I should think you'd like having me around, Carson. Imagine being in this situation without me, at least you have somebody to kick it with."

"What do you want, Muse, I'm not in the mood."

"You're beyond frustrated, I understand. You may as well pick up that pencil over there."

"What, what the…"

"I'd say this could be a hell of a time to get some serious writing done," he said. "Come on, man, it's not like you have a lot of other things going on."

"You actually believe I could focus on writing fiction right now," I said, "and here I thought you understood me pretty well."

"Why not, what else you have to do? And who said it's got to be fiction. Look, Carson, a lot of great writing has come out of places just like this, Mandela, Dr. King, part of the New Testament."

"Boy, and here I thought I was crazy."

"My job, the reason for my existence, is to inspire you to write. I see an opportunity here. In fact I think if you could climb down off that cross for just a bit, you might very well create your

masterpiece, the crowning jewel in your career."

"So you don't think I have cause for distraction and/or

deep, black, depression?"

"Best time for writing in my opinion. Look, so you write a

few words, see if it goes anywhere. You can always flush it down

your little throne over there and get back to the 'woe is me,'

right?"

"Have you ever tried to communicate with her?"

"What?"

"Bianca," I said, "I've been thinking, you said she hates you,

wants you gone. And obviously you know about quite a bit of her

goings on. Yet you've never encountered her?"

"No, I've known of her existence, I knew she was going to

torch your apartment just before it happened. And somehow I

know how she feels about me hanging around, that's it, man."

"They're sending me to Atascadero."

"What?"

"You heard me; we're on our way to the funny farm, my friend."

"But you haven't been convicted of anything," he said, "what the hell is going on, Carson?"

"Frustrating when you don't have access to the whole picture isn't it," I said. "As far as I can tell you live only in the creative part of my imagination, I have a feeling we're about to get a whole lot closer, my friend."

"Hypnosis, you know that's got to be..."

"Court ordered, can't say I'm all that surprised. Just hope, Miss Sybil, is up to it. If the bitch shows up there's a very good chance I won't be tried."

"No, just locked in a padded cell indefinitely," he said, "I don't see such a big difference. You're giving up, Carson; I told you something's not right…"

"Fuck, dude," I said, "you think I'm making choices here?"

"I don't think you killed him. Change that, I know you didn't kill him, and I'm damn close to positive she didn't do it ether."

"What, but…"

"I would know if you or it or whatever-the-fuck had killed somebody, Carson. There's just no way I would not know something like that."

"You know in spite of all this, you're lookin' damn good, man."

"Thanks, Scratch," I said, "man, I've missed you so much. You're even more beautiful than I remembered."

"There's good news," he said. "Derrick's, coming in after me; I'll just say he's on to something big."

"Bullshit, tell me what you know, man!"

"I just know there's something about that woman, the secretary. And I know she's gone, Carson, I mean like, she's really gone."

"Mrs. Shelby, what do you mean, she's gone?"

"Derrick, knows a lot more than I do; I just know that he, the cops or nobody else can find her. Her apartment is cleared out; in fact they can't see that there was ever any furniture moved in there. Just a blow-up mattress and an old piece of shit TV."

"She's probably in a witness protection program."

"Protection from who?" he asked, "You're in here. Anyway, she started working for the doc ten days before you started seeing him, she offers the only eye witness account, turns over the tapes, and now she's gone."

"So what does that say about the case against me?"

"Well, I wouldn't start packing your tooth brush just yet, but... I'm sure, Derrick, will be going over the details. Tell me again about how you can't stop thinking about me. How you're up all night..."

"Okay, wrap it up, Elliot," commanded a voice over an intercom, "transport's here for you."

"What," I asked of the guard behind a second Plexiglas window. "I have another visit coming!"

"Sucks to be you," he said.

The receiver connecting me to Scratch went dead. I placed my hand flat against the window that divided us and mouthed the words, I love you.

Damn, it was scary! Atascadero State Hospital, may as well say, California State Institution for the Criminally Insane. I'll say that at least from the exterior; the buildings did somewhat resemble a hospital. Bars, guards, and razor wire made it perfectly clear exactly what this place was however. I could be here a few weeks, or this might very well be the end of the road for me. I could hear the screaming lunatics before we entered through the first steel door.

No sooner than I placed my bedroll onto the concrete slab and well-worn mattress they called a bed I was called out of the room and shown into a private office. There they sat; my salvation, the site administrator, my attorney Ralph Walberg and Derrick Samuel.

"It's not necessary that you say anything, Mr. Elliot," said Walberg. "We have in our possession a court order that you be released into our custody immediately."

"Huh," I said, "what's happening? You mean I'm..."

"That's right," said Derrick Samuel, "you're coming with us, my friend. We found her."

"Mrs. Shelby," I said, "you mean you found her since I left LA County this morning?"

"Actually the name is, Marsha Holloway," said Samuel. "She's been in custody a few days. So, I see Scratch let the cat out."

"He told me you'd been trying to contact her and that she'd apparently taken off. She is involved?"

"I'll say," said Walberg, "we've got a lot to talk about, Carson, but first let's get you out of here."

The way things were explained to me; first by Derrick and then my attorney. Mary Holloway, had until two years prior been a divorced single mother struggling to raise a mentally disturbed teenaged boy in the suburbs of Seattle, Washington. Her boy,

Shaun Holloway, had taken his parent's divorce extremely hard.

The acting out started just before the legal separation. When his

father, Jack Holloway, announced he was moving to Los Angeles,

Shaun's, acting out turned violent. He was fifteen years old. At

first his cruelty was aimed at smaller, weaker kids at his school,

then for a time directly at his mother, and after that many of the

neighborhood pets were turning up dead. In desperation, before

he was caught and put away; the parents agreed that he should

join his father in L.A. Not a patient man, Jack Holloway, had laid

down firm conditions under which his troubled son would be

allowed to join him. Primary among those conditions was that he

was to see, Dr. Randal Epstein, on a weekly basis. Dr. Epstein had

for a short time been a professor of psychology at UCLA. Jack

Holloway had been among his star students.

At first there was real, noticeable progress. Shaun seemed

to respond well to a combination of medication and talk therapy.

Dr. Epstein was able to help the boy curb his hostility and

aggression towards people and especially small animals. His

continual, steady progress went on for several months. However, when his mother came to L.A. for a short visit she was unimpressed. She knew her son too well, but she had to concede he had become quite the good actor. Perhaps it was only her cursed with the ability to see through his smiling mask of bullshit. After all it was she that he'd come after with a ball-peen hammer, twice! After a few days of tense nearly nonexistent communication between the three of them, she asked that Shaun drive her to the airport two days earlier than planned. Maybe the long drive would be a chance to try to gauge where the boy actually was emotionally. Her son was a dangerous person; she knew that as perhaps no one else on the planet. The things he had done to those poor little animals, and all the horrible sadistic filth she'd found in his computer files after he'd moved out. Just because he was sick, dangerously mentally ill, didn't however mean that she didn't love him. How could she not love him? He was her only child and the only person in her life. She didn't even have a husband any more.

As Shaun closed the driver's seat door of his father's, BMW, Mary noticed the droplets on his long sleeved shirt. When he put his arms up to take the steering wheel a scream rose from deep within her.

"Roll your sleeves up," she'd demanded!

"What, mom?!"

"Get them up, God, damn it," she yelled. "I'll scream, you hear me, Shaun, I'll scream until..."

He did roll them up, and when he did Mary did scream! Her baby, Shaun Holloway's arms looked like ground hamburger meat. The brilliant, Dr. Randel Epstein, had helped her boy by turning his rage and violence onto himself.

"You lookin' good, baby," said Etna, hugging me tight as I came through the door from the garage. Dallas and Skye were next; Etna was in a hugging mood. "Well, I's see they don't feed ya nothin' in dere. Don't worry non Etna know how ta fattin' ya up just right, ha-ha!"

"Good to see you again, Miss Etna," I said. "I have to tell you, I was getting a little worried about never smelling what I smell right now again."

"Nonsense, dat what it is," she said. "Well, I whatin nar bit worried bout dem folk holdin' on ta ya long, baby. No way, no way, dat's what I tells dees two ever day. Dat boy, do somethin' like dat, Etna know, believes me ol' Etna know mo den y'all thank."

"I'm hungry," I said.

"Course, ya are," she said, "well, you right, dat ma special gumbo, fixed up just like you like, Carson Elliot, heavy on the crab and jumbo shrimp. Gon' get yo self cleaned up, cornbread coming out in bout nine minutes."

"Better hurry, man," said Skye, "you know how she is about her bread, its got to be right out of the oven."

"Well, you two been out dere two," she said, "go on clean dem paws fo' ya sit down ma table."

-The doorbell rang-

"Etna take care dat," she said, "now go on, get!"

"Hey baby," it was Scratch. "You didn't think I'd miss this did you?"

I had no words. Everything that had happened over the last three months washed over me in an instant. The tears finally came, held back through most everything; they came in torrents. I cried out loud and hard as I collapsed into my lover's arms. Scratch held me tight as I wept. After just a little while Dallas and Skye joined us. Etna came from the kitchen wiping her hands in her apron. We all held on to each other. No one said a word; in that moment there was nothing to say. This was my family, I loved all these people.

-The doorbell rang again.-

"Now ever body sit down, stop ya wellin'," said Etna; starting for the door, "got two mo folk stoppin' by."

"Pasta," she said; as she opened it, "Pasta Cindy, well y'all come right on in, have a seat. Etna put down two mo' plates."

"No, we can't stay, Etna," said Pastor Cynthia Brown, "we're both speaking in Long Beach tonight."

"Well, come on," said Etna, "preacha' folk in da' house; gotta lease bless the table."

"Hey, Pastor," said Dallas standing; taking the man's hand, then hugging his wife. "Pastor Cindy, this is our friend, Carson."

"The writer." she said; extending her hand, "Finally, we meet. I've been looking forward to this, Carson. You're a great writer."

"Thank you, ma'am," I said. "So you've seen the show? I don't remember..."

"Of course," she said, "opening night. We didn't meet because I had to leave immediately after the curtain. Hey, everybody!"

"You look fabulous pastor," said Dallas. "Of course, that's nothing new."

"Sure you guys can't stay?" asked Skye. "We were just about to dig in."

"No, there's a women's conference in Long Beach," said Pastor Johnny Brown, "I just wanted to stop by and maybe have a quick word with, Carson. You think that would be alright, brother?"

"Sure," I said, "it's good to see you, pastor, thanks for coming down there..."

"You guys can use my office," said Dallas.

"Well, I'm hoping the good Lord will put it on your heart to fix us up just a little small container, Miss Etna," said Pastor Cindy. "What do you think, any chance of that?"

"Got it all packed up; ready ta go," said Etna, "cept, ya know ol' Etna don't believes in no small containas come ta y'all!."

"Congratulations," said Pastor Brown; as the two of us stepped into Dallas's home office. "I hear there's been a full confession."

"That poor woman," I said. "I mean, I know what she did was horrible, unimaginable, but still."

"Admirable that you would still have some compassion after what you've been through," he said. "She was perfectly willing to put you away forever, Carson."

"I guess we'll have to wait for her trial to know the whole story."

"It looks like she needed a patsy to take the blame after she carried out her plan for revenge. She blamed Epstein for her son's rampage and horrific suicide at his school."

"From what I understand, he drenched himself with gasoline and then pointed a shot gun at police," I said. "But, why me pastor?"

"You threatened the man on tape, brother." he answered. "You even said you'd use fire. The woman knew about the arson case up North. Apparently she'd been listening in on his sessions; looking for her fall guy."

"How do you know all this, Pastor Brown?"

"Derrick, was working for me remember. You know all this really doesn't address the real problem though, Carson."

"I did what you asked." I said, "You know that's the only book I could get my hands on in isolation."

"There's got to be a reason for that, right," he said. "Even non-believers have heard the stories. You know I got delivered while in prison myself."

"It was drugs for you."

"Well, that's what I got put away for all right, only the tip of the iceberg though. Man, if I had to pay the price for all of my sins... Well, let's just say, I got off easy. God, is real, Carson."

"Some people might say the real power is in you believing the story," I said.

"And? I don't know about you, brother, but that sounds like a pretty good deal to me. Let me ask you something, brother. If you with your own two eyes saw a dead man brought back to life by; say having his hand placed on this light bulb," he said removing the shade from Dallas's desk lamp, "would that leave an impression on you?"

"Of course," I said, "but I have to be honest with you, Pastor, I'd probably be thinking the man was never really dead.

Maybe the heat from the bulb would have burned his hand;

waking him up."

"That's fair enough. Now let's say we marched in three

blind women. Mind you, these would be women that you knew to

be blind. Let's make them a quartet of singing blind sisters,

Women the whole world knew to be blind. One by one they

touched the bulb."

"I think I see where this is going."

"Stay with me," he said. "What about me? I've written a

little myself, brother. My testimony helped build "One Love." Do I

impress you as a liar?"

"I've read your story, Pastor, and your brother's book," I

said. "I think you're preaching to the choir here. Jesus Christ, is

Lord, I accept that."

"He's the light bulb of the world, brother, "A balm in

Gilead." Please, kneel with me, Carson Elliot."

Timothy Blaine

Chapter Twelve

Her

"Stop it! I mean it!"

"Oh, come on, baby," she said, "what's the matter? You just said you loved me not five minutes ago."

"I don't like the way you're acting right now," said Scratch, "I'm telling you to stop it, Carson! Fuck it, I'm leaving."

"Oh, now don't go hurting my feelings, baby," she said, "I'm just tryin' to whip some of this good lovin' on yo' fine ass."

"Stop talking like that, what's the matter with you, dude?! And what the fuck have you done to your hair?!"

"Sexy huh, you like it, baby?"

"No, I don't like it," yelled Scratch, "if I wanted to be with a fuckin' woman... I don't believe this shit, dude! I feel like I'm in a fuckin' horror movie and your ass is the feature creature!"

"Now, watch your mouth," she said. "Underneath all this beauty, lies a very sensitive woman."

"Fuck you," he yelled, "Where are my damn pants?!"

"YO PANTS ARE RESTIN' IN HELL, MOTHA FUCKA! YOU READY TA GO GETTUM?!"

"What?"

"YOU THINK I'M THE FEATURE CREATURE, HUH," she said picking up a marble table lamp; ripping it from its socket, "PUNK, YOU AIN'T GOT NO IDEA!"

"You're that bitch," he yelled! "You're what they've been talking about!"

"BIANCA THE BEAUTIFUL, NOW GET TA STEPPIN', MOTHA FUCKA," she said taking the first swing, barely missing him and knocking a huge hole in the plaster wall nearest the room's exit. "I FIGURED IT'D BE REAL EASY GETTIN' RID OF YO PUNK ASS!"

Though a very muscular, masculine man, Scratch did run, he ran fast, pants, shoes, and socks all forgotten. After ripping it from the plaster; she threw the motel's marble lamp after him grazing his head.

"AND YOU TELL THAT BOOTLEG PREACHER NOT TO COME AROUND HIM NO MORE! BOTH YOU MOTHA FUCKAS BEEN WARNED!"

I sat staring blankly at Skye as he read over the contract we were both to sign with the touring company that would take "A Perfect Place to Hide," out on the road. We were sitting in his office at Stratton Records. Dallas was busy auditioning women for

a new group he and Scratch were putting together. Scratch

however was a no show, which was from what I understood; way

out of character for him. The man was a textbook workaholic, the

type that rarely missed work and never without calling in.

Something was bothering me, the last thing I remembered about

the night before was checking into that motel on Sunset

Boulevard in Hollywood. We had probably gone through a bottle

of wine at Le' Dome, then at least two cocktails at a gay bar on

Santa Monica Boulevard. This was a lot more than I was used to

drinking.

"Hey, you in there?" said Skye snapping me back into the

present. "Must have been a late night, what time did you get in

anyway, man?"

"Well, the sun wasn't quite up," I said, "I do remember that

much. From now on its two glasses of wine tops for me."

"So, what, you guys have a fight or something?"

"Why do you say that?"

"Well, he didn't show up for auditions this morning for one thing," he said, "second, he's not answering on his cell or home phone."

"I don't remem... I don't think we argued about anything."

"So what happened, Carson, damn. 'Inquiring minds want to know.' It was the first time, right?"

"I don't think things got that far," I said. "I'm worried, Skye, to tell you the truth I remember checking into a motel, and I remember getting into the shower together..."

"Hey, what's up," it was Dallas walking in, "what did you do to my star producer, man?"

"We're worried," I said.

"He's okay," said Dallas, "I just got a call. Kinda vague about why he didn't show up. He asked about you, Carson. Well; he asked if you were here anyway."

"Was it a good 'is he there'?" I asked.

"Hard to say," said Dallas, "what happened, man?"

"I dunno," I said. "C'mon, Dallas, spill it."

"I don't want to get... Look, he told me to call him back after you left. So you can't tell us anything?"

"No, I can't tell you shit, dude," I said standing. "You need me to sign anything else, Skye?"

"No, we're cool," said Skye, "There are a couple issues with the singles, but nothing that can happen right now."

"Okay, so I'll get outta here," I said as my eyes puddled, "you think Henry could drive me back."

"Every couple has problems, Carson," said Dallas, "especially in the beginning. Scratch, is a good dude and he's good for you, man. You guys will work it out."

"I don't even know what the problem is," I said starting for the door. "Fuck, I just want to be a normal person, is that really so much to hope for? Who knows what the hell I've done now."

Pastor Brown asked me to pick up a couple 'po' boys' on my way to 'One Love.' We'd have to have lunch there in his office as he was headed for LAX right after our meeting. I don't know what I was expecting from Pastor Brown. He was a preacher, not a doctor. I only knew I felt safe around him, I felt like the pastor was the only one who truly understood what I was up against.

"Come on in, brother," he said, "you look tired, Carson. You get any sleep?"

"Not much," I said, "probably a little hung over too."

"Look, before we get started you should know I just spoke with, Scratch."

"He was here? Is he here in the building now, pastor?"

"We spoke over the phone," he said. "I know about what happened last night, Carson."

"Great, then you can tell me!"

"Have you ever been to Denver, brother?"

"Huh?"

"Denver Colorado, that's some mighty beautiful country."

"Pastor Brown, if you're trying to tell me you don't have time for this right now I..."

"Well, there's a little truth there," he said biting into his huge sandwich. "Come ride with me."

"To Denver Colorado; just like that?"

"Yeah, we have our own jet. I'll have you back in a few hours, promise."

"I'm so tired, pastor."

"So sleep on the plane," he said taking another bite, "come on, brother, hang out with me a little."

"You're serious?"

"As serious as a man ducking a marble lamp aimed at his head."

"I like him," said the muse.

"Pastor Brown," I said, "yeah he's cool, huh? Well I guess we just figured out one thing for sure. You only live in my subconscious, brother. I've got to be sound asleep right now; we're on a plane and nobody's trippin'."

"I thought we were past all that, Carson."

"I still haven't quite figured you out, but at least I know I'm not sitting here talking to myself."

"So, Scratch, saw her," he said. "They actually talked?"

"More than that," I said, "it looks like the crazy bitch tried to fuck him."

"Damn."

"Damn, is right! Dude, what the hell am I going to do? According to the pastor she got violent. Scratch, won't even talk to me, fuck!"

"I did know about that part," he said, "when she's angry or violent everything goes red. It's how I knew she didn't kill Epstein. We need a plan, Carson; she's getting stronger, bolder."

"Scratch told Pastor Brown that she threatened the both of them if they came around me. I'm scared, Muse."

"The pastor's not intimidated, you've told him everything?"

"The way he sees it, I'd probably benefit more from an exorcism than seeing another shrink. But you're right, Muse, he's not intimidated."

"So what's this trip about?"

"He's preaching somewhere," I said, "next stop, Denver Colorado. This is just another day's work for him. He'll probably be in some other part of the country tomorrow."

"I'm sorry about, Scratch," he said. "I guess cells don't work on planes, but…"

"The phones ring both ways, man. I'm not calling anymore."

"Give him a little time, Carson. I sense he really cares about you and I know you're in love with him. She must have shaken him up pretty bad."

"Yeah, but he knew about… hell, everybody knows about that sick bitch now. Change that, about my sick ass! Maybe I would have been better off staying at Atascadero with all the other nuts. I don't want to talk anymore, Muse."

"So you're fictionalizing your own story," he said. "I think it's a great idea, brother."

"What, you mean you... of course you knew, you're me right?" I answered. "Damn, how did I ever get so fucked up?"

"Well, that gets right to the heart of it doesn't it."

"Come again?"

"Isn't that what drives most psychological splintering," he said, "childhood traumas, forgotten abuses, shit like that?"

"English, English, dammit!"

"It's not going to help you for me to figure it out, Carson. I'm happy about the new story, now like you would prepare for any other good story; do your research, my friend."

"Huh, what do you mean?"

"You know exactly what I mean, dude. Like most of your problems are in your head, so then are your solutions."

"Why is it necessary that you play with me, Muse," I asked? "If you know something that would help me..."

"Due diligence. Research, Carson, research like your life depends on it."

"You're telling me... I know what you're saying. You're telling me; it does."

It was a nice church, not nearly as grand as "One Love," but just as beautiful. I figured it had to have belonged to the Catholics at some point in history. The cathedral ceilings and stained glass windows had been crafted by masters. Whoever was playing on the organ sure was... Oh my God... it was Scratch!

"Okay, so here are the rules," said Pastor Brown. "I'm here only as a mediator. Stay in your seats, nobody runs, one of you will talk while the other one listens, don't talk over each other. If you feel ambushed or tricked, Carson, I apologize. Scratch and I have been on a particularly tight schedule this week; he was flown up here a few hours after you guys saw each other last."

"He knows, or at least I was trying to tell him…" said Scratch.

"Talk directly to Carson, Scratch," said the pastor. "Tell the man how you feel."

"You think I could go first?" I asked facing Pastor Brown, then shifting my gaze to Scratch. "I'm so sorry, brother. It's been one thing after another since the day you met me. I know you didn't sign up for all this, Scratch. Who in their right mind would? Please believe me, I have absolutely no recollection of what happened in that room the other night, still I'm sorry about…"

"I know that," said Scratch. "That wasn't you, Carson."

"I don't know what else to do, man. I've been seeing shrinks since I was a kid, a lot of good it's done me."

"Epstein was getting close to something," he said.

"That worked out real nice."

"Hey, what happened between him and that damaged woman had nothing to do with the work you guys were doing, man! You can't take that onto yourself, Carson, you were a victim there as well."

"Still, she/I threatened him! I've heard that tape, man. I think anybody can see that person is dangerous."

"Tell me about it," he said, "had me running down Sunset Boulevard in my drawers. I'm sorry for shutting down, Carson, I hope you understand when I tell you; first that I'm in love with you…"

"But…"

"Yes, there is a, but. I gotta tell you, I'm scared, Carson. I'm scared because I don't know how to help you, man. I'm scared because I'm a single parent with two kids…"

"Your girls, you couldn't expose them to me, I understand that."

"This is so fucked up," said Scratch. "Pastor; you want to jump in here?"

"I'm a man of faith," said Pastor Brown, "you both know the way I'm going to talk when I start talking."

"So I have a demon; that needs to be cast out," I said. "Sent into a herd of pigs or the fiery pit, something like that?"

"A lot of people take on demons in the course of a lifetime, Carson," said the pastor. "I'm sorry to say that in my experience an awful lot of the transference takes place before ten or twelve years old."

"Transference," said Scratch and me in unison?

"A child's mind is fragile, not fully developed," said Pastor Brown. "It's also a human sponge; absorbing good, bad and evil memories. Sometimes the very worst of those memories get buried."

"Traumas," said Scratch, "demons."

"Demons work in the dark places of the mind," said the pastor. "In order to cast out a demon you must first drag or kick it into the light."

"I have no memories of my life before eight years old," I said. "We don't even have pictures of me before my eighth birthday."

"You mean at your parent's house," asked Scratch.

"I mean nowhere," I said, "not at either of my grandparent's homes, my aunts and uncles, cousins, nowhere. There's not a single baby picture of me anywhere in existence that I'm aware of."

"Then we know where to start," said Pastor Brown. "The plane's leaving in about an hour, so you guy's shouldn't get too hot and heavy with the making up business. I want you to meet with Derrick ASAP, Carson."

"Security," I said.

"Investigator," said Scratch, "Derrick is the best, man. I love my pastor."

"Your parents won't see me," Derrick Samuel informed me over the phone. He was calling from San Francisco. "I spoke with your mom last night; we'd agreed to meet at their apartment this morning, instead I got a call."

"My Dad, the attorney," I said. "They're probably assuming you're somehow involved with the Epstein case. I'll call them the moment we hang up."

"The birth certificate you gave me is a forgery."

"What?"

"I'm just leaving St. Mary's hospital, there's no question about it, Carson. The document is a fake."

"I don't understand," I said. "Why would I have a fake birth certificate?"

"Can I assume you didn't get it directly from the hospital?"

"No, my mom gave me the copy when I was, fifteen, sixteen years old."

"How far do you want to take this, Carson," he asked. "Take a minute before you answer that."

"I don't need to think about anything, man. Let's dig it all up, I need to know the truth; whatever the hell that is. What do you need from me, Derrick?"

"Okay, so let's hold off on contacting your parent's for the moment. I'm going to need a DNA sample from you."

"Huh, what are you...?"

"We need to get our facts straight. I think you understand where this is going, Carson, you're sure you want to do this?"

"You think I was adopted," I said. "You're saying my parents may not be my real..."

"There could be any one of a number of reasons for the birth certificate. All we know for sure is that, for whatever reason, your parents thought it necessary to give you phony papers as a teenager."

"You're going to need theirs as well."

"I'll take care of that," he said, "it's a lot easier than you might think. I'll need the alarm code for the Oakland apartment though."

"There's no alarm there," I said. "What do you mean by... my parents only have one residence, I mean they own quite a few rentals but..."

"I really hate this kinda work sometimes," he said. "Let's just say your dad may not be "working late" as often as he reports. Look, if or when either of your parents calls you, keep it short and sweet. If they ask about me; be vague, it's okay if they start to squirm a little but we don't want to show our hand just yet."

"You think my father's got something going on the side?"

"Probably not related to this case, but you said you wanted a full report, right? Yeah, it looks like he keeps a little love nest up near his office. I have a feeling I won't be finding your mom's DNA there."

"Son of a bitch," I said! "Keep my mom out of it, man. I don't want her finding out about that, at least not from us. If it's any help, she smokes in her car."

"Perfect," he said, "I'll call you when I have more."

"I like it," said my muse, "this detective of yours is no joke."

"He's not wasting any time that's for sure," I said. "How much do you know about me, Muse, about my past? I think it's time we stopped with the games."

"At least as much as you know about yourself. Look, Carson, my thing is your creativity."

"I have a feeling Samuel is about to uncover something big about my past."

"And you're telling me you never suspected," he said. "Come on, man, you don't even resemble ether one of them. That and no memory before eight years old, denial or not…"

"I feel my mind shutting down again," I said. "There's something I won't or can't face."

"You think it's safe to try to navigate this without any help, Carson?"

"You're talking, another shrink, no thank you! A lot of good that's done me, no I'm with Pastor Brown, this is bigger than psychiatry. This Bianca thing is a demon, and it will be dealt with as such."

"You're going to pray her away, that it?"

"Ye of so little faith," I quoted.

I'd taken a little writing studio above 'The Gap' on Hollywood Boulevard; it was a simple space with just enough room for a desk, chair, and single bed. The bathroom was down the hall. I sat and wrote and wrote and sat for weeks after Derrick Samuel was put on the case of uncovering my past. The working title for my fictional story was "Tommy & The Woman." I can't remember a time when the words flowed so easily. Pages and occasionally whole chapters came to me so quickly that I often wondered if it was all just manic gibberish. I resisted the temptation to re-read and edit the chapters as was my usual method; so fearful was I of losing momentum. Though this book was intended to be a novel only inspired by personal events, I was only kidding myself if I thought it not a psychological adventure into my own twisted psyche.

My protagonist's early years strongly resembled my own; at least after the age of eight. Tommy's parents were both doctors at St. Mary's hospital for a time, but after five chapters with no edits I realized I had to go back and change the father's profession to, attorney. I don't know why I thought that detail

vital to the story; but somehow I did. Of course I realized I could

and perhaps should have changed key time frames, locations,

characters and events in order to maintain the cover of fiction;

but I also realized this story was much more than simply

entertainment for my readers, I intended to tell it just the way it

came to me. Amazingly Scratch and I seemed to be growing closer

by the day, how that man was able to look past so much. I

wondered about the others. Granted I'd never been very good at

the dating game, but I was no virgin. There had been a few guys

since I'd become sexually active in my late teens, but now as I

looked back over my life I couldn't recall even one instance, with

the exception of Charlie Franklin, my one and only boyfriend who

had hung around for more than a couple weeks. Now I

remembered a few instances where I was sure I'd made some sort

of connection, but then the dude would abruptly stop calling

and/or stop answering my calls. I always wrote it off to the

fickleness of the gay life. Now I had to wonder as I wrote, was it her? Was it possible that the transformation witnessed by Scratch on that strange night at the motel in Hollywood not an isolated incident? Granted I remembered meeting and occasionally bringing guys back to my apartment, but as far as the actual sex, nothing. Not a single memory of it. I picked up my cell, called Derrick, and gave him Charlie's name and last known address.

"Hey, Carson, come on in," said Skye. "How's the new place?"

"Thank God for flat panel TVs," I said, "or I couldn't have one."

"That small, huh? You know you're welcome to come back, man. Stay as long as you need." We were sitting in his office at Stratton. Dallas was busy in one of the three recording studios.

"Naw, it's cool, perfect for writing. Eventually I'll get a little apartment but I may even try to keep it after I finish the project. It makes me feel like a grown up, like a real writer, you know."

"And how's that going?"

"Fantastic, I'm over two hundred pages in," I said, "I don't think I've ever written this fast or well, man."

"You're still calling it fiction?"

"Hey, man, we never talked about, Epstein. I mean we're the ones that knew him. Skye, I'm so sorry for bringing all this down on that man, his family, and on you, brother."

"Epstein was a good dude," said Skye, "he helped a lot of people, including you and me. You had nothing to do with his death, Carson. Mary Holloway had already wiggled into that job, before you got to town her plan was in motion. If it wasn't you she set her sights on to take the fall it would have been some other innocent."

"How's it going with your dad, man?"

"Actually I was just waiting for Dallas to finish up. My father hung himself this morning, Carson. I got the call about an hour ago."

I stood with my arms out stretched; we held each other tight and long. It had been such an odyssey with Skye's father, Raymond Prescott. The man had killed four people, two of which were totally innocent bystanders. Though, of course no one had dared verbalize this possible outcome, I for one had suspected my friend could receive such a call at any time. Perhaps Mr. Prescott could have survived if it were only his evil wife and her detective/hit man; he had killed, but the servants. The house keeper had practically raised, Skye, and their butler had been with the Prescott family since Raymond's high school years. Using an explosive had been reckless. I was not surprised the man had taken his own life. What surprised me was that it took him so long.

Chapter Thirteen

The Report

"Hey, come on in, Derrick," I said, "sorry I don't have an extra chair."

"Place kinda reminds me of my first dump over on Ivar," said Derrick taking a seat on my half made bed. "We've got a lot to talk about."

"Okay."

"DNA's back, they're your parents all right."

"That's good, right," I said? "Somehow I'm getting a bad vibe from you, man. It's good my parents are who they say they are in relation to me, right?"

"Sure, it's not that," he said. "Look, Carson, something else came up with your DNA."

"Come on, Derrick, loosen up a little, you're freaking me out with the serious mug. I hope you're not about to tell me I'm linked to some crime... I'm not am I? Oh, please tell me I haven't done something."

"No nothing like that. Okay, so here it is, you're DNA is not male, at least not exclusively."

"What?!"

"Lab's repeating the test now."

"What? What the fuck are you talking about, dude?!"

"I have the original certificate of birth, Carson," he said. "You were born hermaphrodite, I think the term is intersexed now."

I sat staring through him; unable to speak.

"The initial surgery was performed soon after your birth, it was..."

"Initial?"

"There were several," he said. "From what I understand it's not uncommon for doctors to choose... You began life as a little girl, Carson."

"Huh, what are you telling me, Derrick? I mean I hear what you're saying, but..."

"You lived as a girl until six years old. Look, I know this is an awful lot to process, we can continue this later if you want."

"Do what later," I said, "go on, finish your story."

"I wish it were only that," he said. "You have an aunt; actually she's your mom's aunt, lives there in the building you once managed."

"Sure, Aunt Gert, actually she lives in the apartment next door to me. We shared a wall. She suffers from Alzheimer's,

Derrick, and she's been clinically paranoid for years. I hope you didn't..."

"Yes, I spoke with her."

"I wish you hadn't done that," I said. "She's just a sick old woman, man."

"Sure I could see that," he said, "the lady's got some problems, no doubt about that. She's convinced the fire in your building was intended for her, or at least her apartment."

"That's crazy; I told you she's..."

"Swears you came banging on her door that day, just before the fire started. She says you half dragged her out of her apartment."

"And you believed her; a sick old paranoid recluse?"

"I took it all with a grain of salt," he said. "I could see she was mixing things up, struggling to stay in the present; until she said something that hit me over the head like a wine bottle."

"Okay, I'm listening, even though I wish you had called me before..."

"She called you, Bianca."

The room fell silent for long moments. "What," I said?

"Not just once, in fact I don't think she ever uttered the name, Carson. Always, Bianca, or, BeBe. I could tell the lady was confused, but why in the hell would she be calling you..."

"She's sick, I told you that. Is there anything else?"

"Yeah, I caught up with that guy, Charlie Franklin," said Derrick, "kinda talkative."

"And?"

"Not a whole lot there, one thing though."

"Okay."

"He told me that in the year or so you guy's dated he never once saw you get an erection."

"Damn!" I said. "They warned me you wouldn't hold any punches. Fuck that asshole, what else have you got about me or my family?"

"Well, let's walk it out, man," he said. "Why a fire, I mean why burn your place down? Let's say there really is this, Bianca, personality; totally separate from you, yet sharing the same body. Why in the hell would either one of you want to torch that place?"

"My heart is palpitating, maybe we should stop."

"And maybe we shouldn't, Carson. I saw your apartment and I saw the arson investigator's report. The accelerant was poured over one wall, the north facing wall, the wall that divided..."

"We lived there," I said in a soft whisper. "That was my family's very first apartment building; my dad won it in a law suit."

"Okay, so..."

"We lived in what is now and has been for many years my, Aunt Gert's, apartment until I was eight years old."

"Finally, real progress," said my muse, "this should have been done years ago, man."

"Maybe," I said. "I'm not asleep, Muse."

"Are you? Well whether a day dream or night vision, this is big, Carson."

"I should be seeing a shrink."

"Really, why," he said? "Look, it's not like you haven't tried psychiatry, man. I hope you see what, Pastor Brown, was saying now."

"About demons?"

"About truth, Carson."

"I've been writing like a mad man," I said, "especially since, Derrick, was here, but then you know that. Things are coming up, Muse. It's not like I remember things then rush to write them down, events are coming to me as I write."

"It's a fascinating story. Bianca, a real person, I mean you actually were, Bianca, for six years?"

"When, Derrick, mentioned that my aunt had referred to me as, BeBe, it was like a bolt of lightning passed through me. Aunt Gert worked for my parents, she was my nanny."

"You remember."

"A little, I remember her," I said, "and I'm starting to get little flashes of my life as a... I remember a little. Thanks for staying on my ass about writing; it's helped me more in these last few weeks than any head doctor has managed in the last few years."

"It's why I was born," he said. "So this aunt, you never visited her?"

"No, like I said; she's a recluse... Okay, so last night I tried something, a little experiment."

"Yeah, I was going to ask you about that."

"So far the fiction has been told in first person," I said. "I couldn't sleep last night, at about 2am I got an idea. I tried writing in another voice."

"Bianca's?"

"I called myself, BeBe, still in first person and well..."

"Well, what? Come on, dude?"

"It's over there," I said pointing at my lap top, "you tell me what that is."

Scratch and I, had been invited by, Skye and Dallas, for a meeting at Stratton before they left for New York the following morning. Though I was trying very hard to maintain my concentration and keep turning out pages, Dallas, made it sound like it was important that the four of us meet.

"Come on in, guys" said Skye, "you're right on time. We've got a few more meetings to get to so let's get down to business."

"Hello, Scratch," said Scratch, "so nice to see you. Thanks for leaving the studio right in the middle of…"

"Mr. Sensitive over here," said Dallas standing to shake our hands, "this won't take but a minute. We've got some great news, guys."

"Okay," I said taking a seat alongside, Scratch, on a little leather sofa.

"Okay, so you need to get an agent, my friend," said Skye, "and quick."

"We've got this friend over at HBO legal," said Dallas. "Well, actually he's more, Skye's…"

"What's going on," said Scratch?

"Well, it's like this, fellas," said Skye, "this guy, Roger Tobin, and I were pretty close friends in high school and well…"

"Come on, Skye, three other meetings, remember," said Dallas. "Okay, bottom line, HBO is interested."

"In the play," I said?

"No, actually according to, Roger, they're interested in the books," said Skye, "all of them. The story is this, Carson; Roger, is an attorney for HBO, works in contracts. A couple days ago he gets assigned to a project developer, guy named, Mike Benet, maybe you've heard of him. Anyway, the dude saw the musical, which had him reading the books; then pitching an idea to the execs for a pilot."

"They're interested in doing a series based on the "Perfect Place" novels," I asked. "You've got to be…"

"Roger, is only called in to put together offers, man," said Skye. "He called to give me a heads up and to get your contact info. This is real, Carson."

"HBO," yelled Scratch, "damn, this could be huge, man!"

"Of course you don't want to talk to anybody directly," said Dallas, "not just yet, anyway. Get yourself an agent, man. That's why we asked both of you in today, you know some people; right, Scratch?"

"Hell yeah," said Scratch, "well mostly music folk, but I know who to talk to."

"Cool," said Skye, "of course you realize if they make you an offer for a pilot, they'll want to option the whole series."

"I think I maybe having a heart attack..." I said clutching my chest, "figure of speech, relax. Fuck, HB fuckin' O!"

"Okay, so we're out of here in the morning," said Skye standing. "We're doing lunch with, Roger, and his wife on Tuesday. I'll flesh out exactly what's going on."

As we stood, Scratch, walked around, Skye's, desk to hug him tight, "I'm real sorry about your dad, brother."

The four of us hugged and held on to each other for several heart felt moments then.

'One Love' was eerily quiet as, Scratch, and I pulled onto the lot nearest, Pastor Brown's, office at a little before 8am on a Monday morning. The pastor had asked to meet with us before we left for San Francisco at noon. I didn't know why the man had taken such an interest in me and my extreme dysfunction. I only knew that I trusted his counsel. Somehow we'd made a deep connection on the very first day I'd laid eyes on him, or maybe it would be more accurate to say since the moment he touched me. The building was dark; we sat in, Scratch's, Benz and waited.

"Does, Pastor Brown, always get this involved with...," I asked, "well let's face it; I'm a total stranger, Scratch. He treats me like I'm a part of his family."

"Well that'd be kinda hard with over 30,000 members. You're right; he's taken a real interest in you right off, my friend. He's even pulled me to the side."

"What do you mean?"

"He was just looking out for you," he said. "It wasn't quite, "So, what are your intentions, young man?" but... Look he just said he could tell things were getting serious between us really quick and that I should understand you're in a very vulnerable place right now."

"Maybe it's you he's looking out for."

"He's looking out for all of us, man. You've heard about, Dwayne?"

"His brother, well I know he was, Joey White's, partner. And I know it was he and, Joey, that build Stratton Records. He was murdered by one of, Joey's, fans right?"

"Yeah, by some stupid obsessed kid," he said, "little bastard actually competed and won a contract with Stratton, what a fucking nightmare. Pastor, and, Joey, took it the hardest of course, but it changed all of us, man. You've noticed all the security over there?"

"Seems like violence has been stalking the company."

"Don't blame Stratton, brother. The company has done well by a lot of people, you and myself included. And just for the record, none of the violence was committed at nor closely associated with the label. We might just as easily say this church was the common denominator. Anyway, since his brother was killed, Pastor Brown, has taken a serious interest in the well-being of everybody connected with Stratton Records. I think he does it in honor of, Dwayne, Carson. It was, Pastor Brown, who took the reins on all that shit two years back; he saved those guys lives, man."

"I thought that was, Derrick."

"Who was working for, Pastor, at "One Love Church." And now; from what you've told me doing a hell of a job for you."

"I'm nervous about confronting them, Scratch," I said abruptly switching gears. "Thank you for coming back with me."

"I love you, Carson," he said; covering my hand with his own. "I hope you understand that doesn't mean I'm going to be in the room with you and your parents."

"I'll handle them. I just need you handy to catch me."

"Well, look who's late for a change," said Scratch gazing into his rear view mirror as, Pastor Brown, pulled onto the lot.

"We've got the whole church praying for you, Carson," said Pastor Brown. "I'm very happy you guys are sticking together and working it out. I'm also happy you're going up there together."

"Actually he's already assured me he won't be a part of the actual confrontation," I said taking Scratch's hand. "He's right of course. I'm so anxious, pastor. A few months ago I'd have started popping the valium by now."

"Well, let's stop and acknowledge, God, right there, brother," said Pastor Brown. "How long without any head drugs, Carson?"

"I stopped taking the meds soon after I got to LA," I said, "it took a couple months. You're right, that is a miracle, I don't even think of them anymore. Well, not until now anyway."

"It's going to be fine, babe," said Scratch, "and you won't be doing this alone. Ain't that right pastor?"

"God is with you, Carson," said the pastor, "I have it on high authority."

"Please don't take this the wrong way, Pastor Brown," I said, "but I've always wanted to ask, somebody. What does that mean exactly?"

"Like the songwriter said, "I've got a feeling, everything is gonna be alright," he said. "Sometimes it's just that simple, brother, a feeling."

"So you guys, preachers I mean, don't actually hear the voice of, God," I said. "No offense, but that's kinda the way it comes across sometimes. Like you guys are saying you hear Him in a way the rest of us don't."

"None taken, I understand what you're saying completely. And then comes the shameless begging and passing the baskets. Folk act like they got to keep you believing they're a conduit to, God Almighty, to keep them baskets filling up. Yep, plenty foolishness in the church you won't catch me denying that, but don't underestimate the power and authority of a feeling, brother. I caught a feeling in a prison cell at San Quentin over forty years ago. I tell you I walked out of that place a free man, brother. Glory to God, even when I tried to fall in the early days of my new life I couldn't, something was keeping me, holding me up. I pray to that 'something,' Carson."

"I've been talking to, God, a lot, Pastor," I said, "and I've been writing like never before. Somehow they seem connected."

A long laugh burst from his mouth.

"That's funny," I asked.

"No, actually that's so wonderful it makes me want to cry," said Pastor Brown. "It's kind of a long story; someday I'll have to tell you about my little brother, Carson. In fact, here," he said handing me one of the books stacked on his desk.

"Dwayne," said Scratch, "yeah, I see what you're thinking, Pastor. Dwayne Brown, wrote directly to, God, since he was a little boy."

"And he got answers," said the pastor. "My brother was a very spiritual man, Carson; long before I had any interest that's for sure. You keep writing brother, I just caught another feeling. Writing may very well be where you'll find your deliverance."

"It's just fiction, Pastor," I said.

"Really," said Scratch, "you're not talking about what you showed me the other day, right?"

"We'd better get to the airport," I said standing. "Thank you for seeing us pastor, I'll try to get him back before Sunday morning."

"We'll manage," he said standing as well, "you guys just do what you have to do. Stay prayed up! Remember to speak from your heart, Carson, and not in your anger.

Chapter Fourteen

Show Down

"You lied to, me," I said loudly, "both of you, how could you keep this from, me? Why? Knowing all the trouble I've been having, how in the hell could you..."

"Are you going to let us say anything," said my father walking over to a little bar cart, pouring at least five fingers of Scotch. "You've been spitting questions at us for twenty minutes. Do you want answers or not, boy?"

"Fine," I said, "just don't lie to me anymore; I can't deal with anymore of your lies. I hope you understand. I'm fighting for my life here. I need real answers. No more bullshit!"

"You're too hard on him, Carson," said my mother. "You've always been so closed to us, to your father especially. You don't understand."

"Why don't we start with my childhood, dad? I don't remember any of it. Change that, I don't remember anything before my eighth birthday. Is that when you gave me a penis? Was it a fucking present?!"

"Oh, shut up, boy," he said, "and lower your voice in my damn house! Sit there and shut up for a while would you?"

"We were in counselling for over two years," she said. "I don't want you to think we came to any decision lightly. We love you, Carson; we love you so much, son, if only you'd let us in."

"It wasn't the first time," said my father after a huge gulp of his very best Scotch. "This thing has been with the, Elliot's, for generations. You said, no more lies, okay. First up, you've always heard that I was an only child. That was a big one. I had two younger brothers, twins, the first one; Zackery, shot himself in the head at fourteen. It seems this piece of shit gym teacher had finally forced him to undress for class. He came home, found my father's .38 and blew his brains out."

"Huh?"

"Tony, was a lot tougher," he said, "he made it all the way to twenty-two."

"Oh, my, God, Dad!"

"Your uncles were intersexed, Carson," said my mother.

"Wait, there's more," he said, "my father's brother, my only uncle."

"No!" burst out of me.

"He lived," he said, "but as a woman, not a very attractive woman. I hear it was heroin for most of his life, but he eventually died of alcoholism. He was homeless the last ten years of his life."

"We did it for you, Carson," said my mother. "Sure we made mistakes, bad decisions, perhaps the worst one being to tamper with your body at all. But you have to know, son, even considering all the deceit, we only did it to protect you."

"I am a man," I said through watering eyes.

"Yes, you are," said my dad. "The first surgery was a mistake. The surgeons had us convinced it was best. It was me, blame me, Carson, your mother wanted to wait."

"By your sixth year it became obvious to us both," she said, "that no matter your biology; you were a boy."

"We couldn't sentence you to live out your life trying to fit a mistake," he said. "It was a very hard decision but one we felt had to be made. There was a second, third and fourth surgery, this time the doctors got it right."

"I blocked it all," I said.

"We were living there in the triangle at the time," she said. "After everything was done we thought it best to not only change your name, but your school and environment as well."

"North Beach," I said, "I remember... something about a big party."

"House warming for the adults," she said, "birthday party for you with a whole new group of kids."

"They were mostly the children of our guests," he said, "all partners or associates of the firm where I worked at the time. You were introduced and have been our son, Carson Elliot, from that point forward."

"My, God, my eighth birthday," I said standing then walking over to gaze out a window. "Up until now, it's been my oldest memory. I buried, Bianca, that day. "

"Both the psychologist and counselor we were working with thought it best to live our lives forward," said my mother. "We didn't keep your pictures, clothes, toys or even a stick of furniture from the old apartment."

"My, God, you took, Aunt Gert, from me."

"Gert, couldn't or wouldn't accept the change. To her you'd always be her little, BeBe. We did what we thought was best at the time, son," said my father. "We let your aunt keep the apartment for as long as she wanted to live there, but well... you were an adult before you saw her again, Carson."

"The fire," I said, "what was that all about? Something tells me you know, even though it was her..."

"You're talking in third person again, Carson," said my mother, "Maybe you're assuming we know a lot more than we do? We haven't wanted to push. What's been happening here lately son, please tell us. "

"You know about, Epstein," I said. "What else do you know?"

"We haven't wanted to push," she repeated. "Oh, Carson, please..."

"He was helping me," I said, "he got a little too close. Look, you know I had nothing to do with the man's death. I was completely vindicated on that. But there was a reason that woman thought she could pin it on me."

"That fucking tape," said my dad laying his face into his hands, "I heard…"

"Then you know," I said.

"He knows what, dammit," she yelled whipping her head to face him, "I've had enough of this, what the hell's been happening?!"

"Epstein, confronted, BeBe," I said, "tell her dad."

"What!" She said, "what the…"

"You really don't know do you, mom? Tell her what you heard on the tape, dad."

"I couldn't get access to something like that, Carson. All I heard was what your attorney told me second hand. You need to be seeing someone, son," he said. "This is not the way to do it; we need to get you the right…"

"No more fuckin' doctors," I yelled! "Tell your wife what you've created! My, God, man, are you always a lawyer?! Tell her… Fine, let me. Your little, Bianca, or maybe you called her, BeBe, as well, is not dead, mother."

"Huh, what," she stammered, "what are you…"

"Let the boy talk," snapped my dad!

"Dissociative identity disorder," I said, "otherwise known as a multiple personality. In other words, I'm outrageously fucked up, mother."

"Oh, my, God," she yelled, "my, baby."

"Your baby 'what' is the question," I said. "Damn, what were you guys thinking?"

"We were thinking we didn't want you hurting yourself," said my dad, "or hating yourself, or being abused…"

"You were afraid I'd kill myself," I said. "You were afraid I'd end up like your brothers."

"Or my uncle," he said tears running freely down his face. I was thirty five years old and that was the first and only time I'd ever seen my father cry.

"It's so beautiful here," said Scratch, "I always loved this city, so different from LA."

"They've got palm trees in common," I said. We'd just left the F-train on Market Street heading for Fisherman's Warf for seafood.

"Well, there's that," he said. "What a great place to grow up, Carson, don't you miss it?"

"Sure, I miss the city a little, but hey, it's just a few bucks away, right? Besides LA has you, "beauty is in the eye of the beholder."

"You know I'd pretty much given up on ever finding love," he said. "You're the only man I've ever loved, Carson; I want you to know that."

"But not the only person," I said. "You must have loved the girl's mom. Tell me about her, Scratch."

"Jenny, oh hell no, that is one crazy... ah, I mean..."

"You can say the word crazy around me, man."

"Naw, well let's just say, Miss Jennifer Wilcox, has a very dynamic personality. We were never really together... I mean we lived in the same place for a while but..."

"She got pregnant," I said, "twice. Now how does that happen?"

"Look, Carson, I've always known I was gay, alright. Granted it's taken me a while... well if you hadn't come along, my friend."

"So I brought you out of the closet?"

"I wasn't in the closet... Well not totally anyway. I've just had a very busy life, man."

"You've been too busy to be gay," I chuckled, "now that's a new one."

"Jenny and I were at UCLA together," he said. "I was nineteen and already working with "Stratton" and "One Love" my freshman year. She'd been married and had a pretty decent career in advertising before her husband took off with a twenty year old stewardess. She'd come back to school to finish up her degree."

"In other words she's older than you."

"Bingo, she was almost thirty when we met. Her ex hadn't wanted kids. I'll give her one thing, she was honest with me. I mean she could have easily tricked me out of my sperm, right? I still remember her pitch, "Honey, my bio clock is running out and I don't have time to find a husband."

"Damn, not shy, huh?"

"As it turns out, I wanted kids too. My nineteen year old mind was working overtime trying to convince me I'd never have any because I was homosexual."

"I'm starting to see the busy-ness."

"My career took off while I was at UCLA full time," he said, "in fact I'd already charted with a group I put together in high school. Then along came the first little princess. We both agreed we should live together to share the responsibilities. Well, one thing lead to another and a year later, Jennifer, was pregnant again."

"An accident?"

"No, like she said; her baby making clock was running out. We'd both been 'only kids,' we didn't want to do that to our baby."

"Sounds rational to me," I said, "so what makes this lady crazy?"

"Now that's a long story, and it's too beautiful a day. Let's talk about us."

"Okay."

"I'm glad we came here, man. Thanks for bringing me along. It's great to see where you were born, where you lived your young life."

"They want to meet you," I said, "my mom especially."

"What?"

"You heard me, besides I want you to meet them, babe. Who knows the next time we'll make it up here?"

"You don't think the timing is a little off?"

"Look 'the gay' hasn't been an issue with us for years if that's what you're thinking," I said. "After the big talk I told them about you. I told them I was in love, Scratch."

"That must have sat real nice with, 'The Republican.'

"Actually, he'd already figured it out; called you "the visiting room guy." Look, it'll be fine, Scratch. They're not bad people. I don't agree with what they did but I understand it a lot better now. They figured or at least hoped I'd have a better chance at a normal life if I never knew the truth. The real curse on the, Elliot's, wasn't that some of the men were born intersexed. What terrified my parents was the family's propensity for suicide. My dad confessed that even though now-a-days you can get a full family history with a few clicks on a mouse, he hadn't once dared, so fearful of what he'd find."

"I think I may have something significant to add to the conversation, Carson," he said. "Oh, man, I wish you would at least consider doing this with a professional."

"Just say what you want to say, babe," I said, "I know you love me and only want to help me."

"Well, it's just something about that night at the motel. You'd had a few drinks, but my head was clear, I'd only drunk

294

Calistoga that night. I'd had that plane to Colorado to catch first thing the next morning."

"Okay."

"We were having a great time, man. Just hanging out, talking, and making out a little. I remember getting in the shower together, actually you were in there first. I joined you. Everything was still great, we started making out in there again, I remember the very instant everything went strange, Carson. I turned the water off; as the steam dissipated I started drying you off. I noticed something on your dick, figuring it was fiber or something from the towel; I bent over to look a little closer. You pushed away from me, and that's when everything..."

"Son-of-a-bitch!"

"Huh, wha... I was just trying to hel..."

"You saw the scarring." I said. It was becoming clear to me now. "That's what it was! That's exactly what it was, son-of-a-fuckin'-bitch! That's what set her off, man."

"That's what I'm thinking too."

"In, Epstein's, office, the last thing I remember before blacking out or whatever was refusing to be hypnotized. He was getting close…"

"She doesn't want you to remember, Carson, she's protecting herself."

"Oh, my, God! The fire! My Aunt was right; it wasn't my apartment she was trying to destroy. Bianca, lived out her entire life in that apartment; she was trying to destroy evidence, Scratch! For whatever reason unlocking my memory threatens her."

"No doubt that apartment would hold a lot of memories."

"Still does," I said. "Are you thinking what I'm thinking, Scratch?"

"Yeah, let's get over there, man."

"Are you scared?" asked Scratch as we sat on the bed of my early childhood.

My Great Aunt had been moved into a very nice nursing facility after the fire. Though there was little damage caused by the blaze next door, my parents had made the decision. Gert had to be getting close to ninety years old. Live-in help and all my drama aside, it was time. It appeared most of the apartment hadn't been touched since the time my family had lived there twenty-seven years earlier. Everything down to the wallpaper, cracking linoleum floors and princess telephones was old, yellowed, dusty. The window coverings which I'd never once seen opened, were all but falling off their rods. Now as we sat together in my bedroom, Bianca Elliot's, room, the man wanted to know if I was scared.

"Of course," I said reaching into my jacket pocket, "Scratch, I don't want to argue about this, take it."

"What, what the hell is that?"

"It's just what it looks like."

"A fuckin' Taser! You want me to…"

"I want you to be safe," I said holding the gadget out towards him, "it won't kill me."

"I know it won't," he said, "because I'm not using it! Let's just go back to LA, man. This is crazy, Carson; we're not qualified for something like…"

"You promised."

"I said I'd come here with you. You've hardly looked around the place, man. Fuck it, we tried, nothing happened."

"We're not leaving this apartment until…"

"Fine," he said snatching it from my hand "doesn't mean I'm using it."

"Thank you; now let's see if we can find some clean sheets. Thank you for doing this for me, Scratch."

"Of course the old darling wouldn't have cable?"

"Not likely; but there's Wi-Fi in the building," I said. "I'll be writing, just be sure you don't close or move my laptop if I doze off or step away. The web cam is recording. Remember babe, if anything happens, try to keep her engaged."

"Tell me again what we hope to accomplish."

"It's not about what we want, Scratch. Let's make this all about, Bianca. Let's find out what she wants for a change. I'm kinda getting the feeling that's a big part of this."

"Come again?"

"Think about it, man. Try to look at this thing from the other perspective."

"You just lost me," he said. "I mean I know your hoping for some kind of theatrical confrontation, a coming together or whatever the fuck..."

"Oh, come on brother you can do this," came a slightly different voice, *"you guys are so close, man. Carson, really, really needs you to focus up right now, brother."*

"What? Carson, you okay," yelled Scratch?!, "Carson..."

"He's fine," said my muse, *"it's starting, don't panic."*

"What the... who are you? What's starting?"

"Maybe he never told you about me. Now before you whip out that Taser, I'm, Carson's, muse, I would never hurt him, or you."

"The dream, dude," said Scratch, "you mean you're real too? You're a separate personality?"

"It's complicated," said the muse, *"this is a learning curve for all of us, man. I've never talked to another person. So you do know about me?"*

"Of course I know about you, you're the one that started all this shit. I know about the concourse, you moving downstairs,

Epstein's, office, fuck, you're the reason he started seeing the man!"

"Trust me, little, Miss Bianca Elliot, had been around long before I showed up. It's funny, sometimes it feels like I'm aware of everything he says, thinks or sees. But it's really just in fragments; my place is in his imagination. He's deeply in love with you, Scratch, don't bail on him. I have a feeling things are about to change."

"I'm not going anywhere."

"So what's the plan?"

"You mean you don't know," said Scratch? "Right, so you only know what you know. We're going to try to force her out, talk to her, something, I don't know exactly."

"And how will you do that?"

"Carson, thinks... well... look, Muse, I hope we'll have some privacy... know what I mean."

"You're going to try to do it aren't you? Damn, you think you'll be able to get it up? Talk about pressure."

"Not if I think you're hanging around, that's for sure."

"He's only got one body, man. Guess that means you'll be fucking all three of us lol..."

"Have you ever communicated with her, Muse?"

"Trust me, if she could kill me without killing him, my ass would have been grass a long time ago."

"So the answer is no?"

"Sometimes I'm aware of what she does or thinks about doing, but no, no communication."

"Are we finished?"

"You really should have that thing a lot handier," he said nodding towards the gadget on the night stand on the other side of the room, "that's what the little cord around the handle is for."

"I'm not..."

"Get the damn thing, man. Keep it on you."

And so it went, one day morphed into two, then three, and then a week had passed, nothing! Scratch and I spent most of our time in the nude. Me, at a little writing desk, him on the bed or floor working on new material for one or more of his many projects. Nothing happened. Absolutely nothing out of the ordinary; well there was that thing between, Scratch, and my muse. That, I liked. There was a time while, Scratch, was giving me the 'full examination,' that I felt certain I was losing consciousness. Turns out it was a false alarm, no, Bianca. We tried calling her out, meditation, lots of wild sex, nothing. I even came across boxes of her clothes, little shoes and dolls stacked in a hall closet; still she remained a no show. As to the work, I was turning out pages so fast I could no longer tell what was fiction and what was memory. As to memory, it was back, for the first time I remembered my life in that apartment, I remembered a lot, I even remembered when the doctors started cutting on me.

"You've got a beautiful place," said Scratch upon entering my parent's downtown Oakland penthouse.

"Thank you!" answered my mother. "Wish I could say I did it all myself. So nice to finally meet you, Scratch. Is that really your name?"

He leaned over to whisper something in her ear.

"Why are you whispering, Helmut," I said with a chuckle. "He had it legally changed, mom."

"Scratch, it is then." she said. "Your father will be down in a minute, Carson. He's on a conference call with the office in London. Why don't you fix our guest and I a drink? I'll have a screwdriver, honey."

As the three of us stepped into the spacious two story great room, my father joined us from another entrance. "So we meet again," he said extending a hand to, Scratch. "Thank, God, it's under so much better circumstances. Carson, you're looking good, son."

"Sorry, it's taken a few days to get over here," I said walking over to the bar cart, "I've been showing Scratch around San Francisco."

"First time in the city, young man," asked my dad.

"No, my parents used to bring me," said Scratch. "I was born and raised in LA, sir. First time with, Carson, though, he gave me the real tour. I've got a new appreciation."

"We love 'The City' as well," said my mother, "who knows, maybe we'll move back some day. We've got a few properties on that side of the bay."

"He knows," I said, "actually we've been staying at the triangle property this week."

"What, in all that mess," said my father, "the place is boarded up for, Christ, sakes, Carson."

"We've been staying in, Aunt Gert's, place, dad," I said, "I've still got all my keys."

"But why..." said my mother, "why would you want to..."

"I remember, mom," I said, "it's okay. I mean it's really, really, alright. Dad, relax, my memory is coming back, no hypnosis, no shrinks, no nothing. It's just about me facing the truth, that's all that seems to be helping me."

"We're so sorry, baby," mom replied with anguish in her voice.

"I know that, mom. Look, I've been doing a little research, mostly on the web or YouTube. It's not uncommon for parents to withhold it from the child for as long as possible. In fact even today many doctors advise it. You did what you thought was best, I accept that. I'm really sorry about your brothers, dad. Now please, no more secrets. Is there anything else?"

"Well, maybe," she said leaving the room.

"So I hear you're a big record producer, Scratch," said my dad. "Anything I might have heard of?"

"Do you listen to gospel music, sir," asked Scratch.

"Oh, he never misses the Grammys," I said. "Scratch produced "The City" album, dad. He works with, Dallas and Skye, on most of their projects."

"A Stratton man," said my dad, "that's a great album, brother. We have it of course. So you and those two are pretty close then?"

"Yeah, we're all good friends," said Scratch. "Just wish I could have been in on "The Perfect Place" project. Those singles are hot 'as is' though."

My mom walked back into the room carrying two large photo albums. "I'm sure you've guessed what these are," she stated. "Are you ready for this, son?"

"I've seen some of her things, mom, sat on her little bed," I said getting a little anxious. "I've even finally acknowledged my scarring for what it is. Actually I think I may eventually find it kinda funny that I had somehow convinced myself I'd been mauled by a big dog..."

"Toby," said my dad, "my, God, you remember that!"

"Toby was a neighbor's bull dog," she said. "Yes it happened, but not 'down there.' The dog attacked you as an infant, Carson. He grabbed your leg through your playpen. The bites were on your leg and foot."

Instinctively I grabbed my pant leg; pulling it up and my sock down exposing the faint scars to Scratch and my dad. "I had convinced myself a dog had chewed on my penis. I've never had an erection."

"This was taken on the day we brought you home baby," she said opening the first album.

As the plane lifted from the runway I pulled my laptop from my carry-on.

"You've got to be kidding," said Scratch. "Come on, Carson."

"Sorry babe," I said, "I've got a lot to get down."

"You mean there's more? Did you even go to sleep last night?"

"I got a couple hours. The muse man is going to be very pleased with me. I finished three chapters in eight days, Scratch. Yep, he's going to be happy with me alright!"

"I think that's about the strangest thing I've ever experienced, talking to him I mean. Of course I know that was you; still... well, it was just weird, man."

"Weirder than your little encounter with the disgruntled feline?"

"Okay, so that was a lot weirder," he said. "You think she's really gone, Carson?"

"I may be the wrong one to ask, I didn't even know she existed."

"Okay, so go to sleep and ask your muse if, Miss BeBe, is still hanging around."

"I feel good, Scratch," I said, "I don't think I've ever felt as good as I do right now. Thank you for doing this with me."

"And thank you for trusting me and letting me into your world, Carson. I love you."

"I'm sure the Stratton folks are rightly pissed off. How many people are we holding up right now?"

"I've got a little catching up to do," he said. "I wouldn't have traded this for the world, man. So, are you going to stop calling the man 'The Republican' now?"

"Poor guy, yeah, I've been kinda rough on both of them. So now you've met the folks, what did you think?"

"I think you guys have been through a lot, man. And I gotta say, Carson, I kinda get their side of it. With all that went on in your father's family, who wouldn't be afraid? You didn't turn out too bad! You're beautiful, masculine, talented and smart. In spite of everything that's happened recently there's nothing suicidal about you, brother. And now you have me, what more could a man ask for?"

I clicked on my email inbox, "Well damn," I said aloud then turned the screen to face him.

"Fuck, dude!"

The last entry was from the New York offices of HBO, subject marked, URGENT.

Chapter Fifteen

It Wasn't Our Fault

[Finished - One] were the words I typed at the end of the last page. This was the way I always ended my first drafts. Now as I sat at my desk staring out onto Hollywood Boulevard, I pondered my next move. I was now under contract with HBO to produce the entire six "Perfect Place," novels over the next three months, the last of which being less than half finished. With the musical still touring and the single, 'We've Done Something Bad' climbing three charts simultaneously, well let's just say, "My cup runneth over." For the first time in the eleven years I'd been writing I was actually making a living. Who would have guessed it'd come from work I'd begun as a homeless twenty something eleven years back. I gotta say, I'm feeling a little "Noah," As if all those years I was building an ark not knowing how or if it would ever sail, now comes the flood. Of course I have to finish that last novel in the series first; even though it'll be crushed into bite sized pieces, and could possibly never make it past the pilot episode. Frankly, I just want to get the thing done! I'm so excited about the new book! That's where my heart and head are now. That damn muse, he had to know where this was going all along...

"Really," he said, "so now I'm a fortune teller."

"Hello, handsome," I said, "I was just thinking good thoughts about you."

"I really think she's gone, Carson, I'm not sensing anything."

"No, I've been sleeping over at Scratch's place most nights. If she was going to show up, I think she would have done it by now."

"When are his kids coming?"

"School will be over in a couple weeks. He'll have them the whole summer."

"So what's the plan?"

"As far as his girls, sure I'll meet them. I won't be staying over there though, that wouldn't be right."

"Hard to imagine you both squeezing in here," he said, "I mean it's great for writing and all, but..."

"We're looking for a place Muse," I said. "Scratch and I are going to live together, buy a little place I mean."

"I figured that. Well, I guess this will be our little spot then, my place is with the work you know."

"Why, you've actually spoken to him. Talk about stranger than fiction, what was that like for you?"

"Since I live only in your subconscious you mean, yeah, go figure," he said. "Well if BeBe can split and make an occasional appearance I guess it would kinda follow, we're both a part of you after all."

"How's the new book coming along, Carson?"

"Just finished the first draft, you must know that."

"Don't assume, brother. Its good work, I do know that. How much longer?"

"That's the thing, I've got to put it down for a while," I said. "I need to close out the 'Perfect Place' series. This HBO thing could be huge, Muse. But even if it's not picked up, my contract is for all six books."

"You're going to be rich."

"No, I'm selling the story. If anybody gets rich off those books, it'll be them. They're taking all the risk, right. Skye and Dallas convinced me to have my agent insist on attaching my name to the title and they actually went for it. It'll read something like "Carson Elliot's – Perfect Place to Hide.""

"Okay, I get it. This series will make you famous."

"If the pilot is successful, yeah, probably a little. Either way, I'll have the money to invest in a new place with Scratch as soon as I turn over the last book."

"It's all coming together, man," he said. "I have a fear, Carson, it's about our relationship. Should I tell you..."

"No, don't," I said.

"Well, come on in, baby," said Miss Etna answering the door, "woo, you lookin' good baby! Where's, Scratch?"

"Working. He sends his apologies," I said.

"He da' one ain't he, Carson, da' one touch yo heart hard I mean?"

"Yeah, he makes me happy, Etna. Where are the guys?"

"Just called; runnin' late. Etna had 'em stop at da' grocery sto' too. Don't fret dey be here soon 'nough. Give us a chance catch up some. Come on back in ma kitchen baby. Look at this big ol' fish I's fixin' up."

"Wow, now that's what I'd call a big fish. What is he, Etna?"

"Albacore, just 'bout ready fo da' oven. So tell me bout dat ol' crazy wainch, baby. Boys tell me she gone now."

"It's been quite a year, I'll tell you that."

"Crazy ol' fool, threatin' and scurin' folk half ta death, need be shame!"

"I've been working on telling her side of the..."

"Etna wouldn't waste her time, baby," she said slamming one of her pots into the sink, "some thangs just plain evil what dey is!"

"It's a little more complicated than that, actually it's a lot more..."

"Let you tell it, well guess the main thang is the wainch got sent right back to da same hell warst she came."

"WATCH YOUR MOUTH, CRUSTY OLD BITCH! BE A SHAME IF THAT NASTY ASS APRON CAUGHT FIRE!"

When Etna Jackson spun around she was holding the ten pound albacore by its tail. POW! Came the first slap across the face, followed by a quick combination to the top of the head. "Get up wainch," Etna yelled, "I ain't scurd none ya!"

As Bianca rose from the floor, POW! Came another blow to the side of the head. "What's da' matta' wit cha, wainch, ain't cha got no fight in ya?! Get up! Ya scurd a ol' woman and a fish?!"

"Stop it," said Bianca starting to get up then falling back to the slippery kitchen floor, she was crying.

"What, what dis here," said Etna, "ya cryin', gal? What ya cryin' fo, spose ta be tough, gon kill ever body, burn ever thang up."

"Just stop hitting me. You don't understand."

"I's understand ya wrong, now wrong is wrong, ya ain't spose ta be. And ya ain't got no call be treatin' dat boy like dat."

"You talk like we're two separate people," said Bianca scooting up against the kitchen cabinets.

"Ain't cha?"

"You've heard about our birth?"

"Etna, know a little."

"You think it was right, what they did to me," said Bianca? "I mean to erase my life, go on like I never existed, is that right?"

"Well, get on up," said Etna offering her hand. "I's wonna hear what ya gotta say. Don't cha start yellin', screamin' at me doh, else I gotta use ma big skillet on ya."

Bianca declined her hand up. "We're not two separate people, or at least we weren't. I've never blamed, Carson, I've just been afraid of dying, old lady; you must know what that feels like."

"Reckon you best call me, Etna. Kill da' old lady stuff! Well, whatcha spec from folk, gal? Dis here a lot ta take in. Ya spec our Carson live like two folk, dat it?"

"I'm getting weaker, so weak," said Bianca. "I've been trying to come out for weeks, I'm dying, Etna."

"Lord, dis a lot ta try understand. Well, I's sorry fo hittin' ya wit da big fish, gal, reckon Etna got a little meanness down deep. Why ya always tryin' ta scure folk?"

"It takes a lot to work up enough power to break through. Only way to get out is to come out screaming. Guess you shouldn't have been calling me names."

"Etna ain't call ya..."

"Wainch, crazy fool, plain evil."

"Oh, okay, well maybe we both need take a little blame. Do seem kinda weak gal, fish knock ya clear off ya feet. Tell ol' Etna what ta do ta hope ya?"

"Tell, Carson, I love him. You tell him, I'm at peace and he shouldn't worry about me."

"Ya mean ya got no way ta commune wit' him?"

"I love him, Etna," said Bianca, "please tell him that. I won't be causing him any more grief. Tell him I'm sorry, Etna. It wasn't our fault.

"Damn," said Dallas upon stepping into the kitchen, "what happened to your face, Carson?!"

I didn't answer.

"Etna, what's going on," he said, "what's wrong with him, what's happened?"

"Po baby," said Etna, "musta slip on a piece a ma fish, look like he a little dazed."

I said nothing; I sat there on the greasy kitchen floor in a trance.

"Maybe he hit his head," said Dallas dialing three digits into his cell.

"No, don't do that," I said softly, "just give me a minute."

"Oh God, Carson," yelled Skye coming in with groceries.

"Watch da floor, baby," said Etna pulling a roll of paper towels from its holder.

"Okay, everybody just stop moving for a minute," I said getting to my feet, "you're making me dizzy. Real sorry about the mess, guys, ah… Miss Etna, can I have a word?"

"Sho'nuff, baby," she said, "just let me clean up dis…"

"No," I said taking her by the arm and leading her towards the den. "We'll be right back, guys."

As the door closed behind us, "You slapped me with that fish, Etna."

"Yeah, three, fo, times," she said, "I'm sorry, baby, weren't you I's swangin' on."

"Okay, so tell me. Tell me exactly what happened in there, Etna."

"It's a lot, baby. First off, gotta say; Etna wrong bout dat gal, otha person ya know. She ain't all bad; she ain't even tough like she pop off at da mouth."

"You talked with, Bianca. But why the fish, Etna, she tried to hurt you?"

"Didn't give her no chance," she said. "You forgive dat gal, Carson, forgive dat part ya self."

"What, I don't blame, Bianca. It wasn't her fault."

"Dat's what she say, gal say it weren't neda one ya fault, I spose ta tell ya dat. And I's spose ta tell ya she at peace. No need ta worry none bout her. She ain't gon bother ya no mo. Well, I don't think she can, Carson. I thank dat gal just died out dere on da kitchen flo."

"That's why she came out," I said. "This was goodbye."

"She tell Etna she barely able get out she so weak. Main thang I spose tell ya, baby. Gal say she love ya, Carson."

"So what do you think, Muse," I asked.

"Well, she's gone alright," he said. "It's like your aura is a hundred pounds and a hundred tints lighter."

"You know that's kinda the way I feel. It's a little sad in a way don't you think?"

"Nope, look it's something that had to happen, man. For what it's worth; I wouldn't say she died. My guess, it's much more like Bianca got absorbed. The more you confronted the truth, the stronger you got. Subsequently she got weaker, but I think she'd need a separate body to actually die. Maybe you should think of it as a kind of merger, big company absorbs a little company, they become one."

"Very good, Muse," I said, "I can live with that. You know you're a really smart du... well you're very smart. And I'm really happy you showed up, promise you'll never leave me."

There is silence.

"Muse?"

A long silence and then; "Carson, my work is done."

"What?!"

"On March 15, 2013 at 10:37 pm, a prayer was heard," he said, "maybe you don't remember. There were so many from you around that time. This one touched the heart of, God."

"You're telling me you're leaving me?"

"Has to happen. Let me see if I can paraphrase; 'Oh God, help me. I wrote one sentence this morning; I don't think I can keep it. Yesterday was no better; nor the day before, nor... God, I'm more than simply blocked; I can't write. Two days ago I got yet another royalty check for less than twenty dollars. Ten years, five books and still I can't cover the cost of ink and paper. I'm embarrassed to cash the checks, Lord; paranoid the tellers laugh as I leave the bank. I'm increasingly embarrassed to call myself a writer. How can I go on doing this, Lord. Obviously no one wants to read what I write. Help me, oh God, I beg you, without the words I have no identity, no purpose, no place of refuge. As to love, I won't bore you with that anymore; it's become a stale joke, who could ever love me? Please consider me, my God, please. Amen.'

"Wow," I said!

"He loves you, Carson," said the muse, "go forth and do great things. Never forget what the Lord has done."

"Muse, Muse, hey come on, man! Spider?"

"Wake up, babe," said Scratch shaking me gently. "That must have been some dream; you knocked me off the bed."

"Not so hard to do on this thing," I said. "Boy, I hope we find a place soon. First thing we're getting together is a big ol' grand California King."

"Actually that's something we need to talk about, about the new place and all that I mean."

"You mean what? Oh God, don't tell me you're… We're looking for a place right, I mean I think that's what we've been doing."

"I don't think I can do it, Carson."

"What?"

"Come on man, live in sin. I'm a father, what kind of example…" he said reaching under my pillow. "I can't do it."

"You can't do what? What the fuck are you…"

Scratch then slid off the bed and onto one knee, "I want it to be forever, Carson," he said, "please, I beg you, please marry me?"

The diamonds and gems were the colors of the rainbow, as were the glistening tears in my man's eyes.

THE END

ABOUT THE AUTHOR

Timothy Blaine is the author of one book of non-fiction "Meth Monster" and three novels in his "Love & Gospel Music" series. "Love & Gospel Music: What's wrong wit' tellin' the damn truth" "The Epiphani" and "Muse." – He lives in San Francisco with his dog, Jimmy.